Canine Contentment
The Essential Guide

Charlotte Garner

Copyright

Disclaimer

Contents

About The Author

Charlotte has been immersed in the animal world from her very early childhood and was lucky enough to grow up surrounded by a vast menagerie of pets including; cats, guinea pigs, hamsters, rabbits, chickens, fish, horses and of course dogs!

Her love of dogs became so strong in fact, that at the age of 11 she actually borrowed a local dog trainer's dogs, in order to attend obedience and agility classes with them, as she did not currently have a dog of her own! It is here where she was introduced to positive reinforcement training and so her dog training obsession began. This arrangement continued for around 3 years, which provided Charlotte with time to gain invaluable skills and experience through working with these dogs, as well as offering the opportunity for her to regularly compete in agility, breed shows and obedience competitions all over the country. It was then, that her trainer and mentor organised for her to have a dog of her own, in the form of Sky, a Border Collie puppy, who is featured on the books front cover. After all, she is the dog that started it all!

Fast forward a couple of years later, to when

Charlotte and her Mum set up their own foster based dog rescue, subsequently acquiring a further 3 dogs in the process, Tizzy, Inka and then later Delta who make up the current 4 dogs that Charlotte shares her life with today, each of whom have taught her countless lessons of their own. Over the years that the rescue was in operation, they helped to rehome over 600 dogs to their forever homes, which was not only a huge achievement, but it also provided Charlotte with numerous opportunities to work with dogs from a whole host of different backgrounds, broadening her experience further still.

Charlotte's love of animals and thirst for knowledge then led her to go on to qualify as a Veterinary Care Assistant, then furthermore gain a diploma in Canine Behaviour, enabling her then set up her own business offering 1-2-1 canine behaviour consultations, as well as group classes for puppies and adult dogs.

Currently, Charlotte runs her own online dog treat business, 'The Natural Snack Pack,' offering natural dog treats and other eco-friendly dog products. She is still as passionate today as ever, about improving the relationship between dogs and owners and in turn, ensuring that dog's lives are happier and more contented.

She describes this book as being 'essentially the

contents of my mind written onto paper, so I am hugely excited to share this with you all in my first book. My love and passion for dogs is so strong, so I am keen to share my knowledge and ethics to the rest of the world, so as many people as possible are able to ensure their dogs are happy, loved and well taken care of.'

Introduction

Our dogs are sentient beings who have the ability to form strong bonds with us as humans and in turn, they look to us to provide them with everything they require to lead a happy and fulfilled life. A good starting point for what your dog requires in order for them to live comfortably, can be found outlined in the 'Five Freedoms' which details a list of five basic requirements which all dogs should be provided with. The standards included in this list are not only something all of our dogs should have as a minimum; they are also a legality in UK law under the Animal Welfare Act of 2006, so failure to provide them effectively is a criminal offence. The 'Five Freedoms' are as follows;

- **Freedom from hunger and thirst -** through the provision of easily accessible clean water and an appropriate diet to maintain optimum health
- **Freedom from pain, injury, disease or illness -** through rapid diagnosis and treatment of any suspected health issues
- **Freedom to express normal, species appropriate behaviours -** through providing a suitable living environment, appropriate facilities and the company of the

animal's own kind if this is appropriate to their individual needs

- **Freedom from discomfort -** through providing a comfortable resting area and shelter from the outside elements
- **Freedom from fear or distress -** through ensuring that the conditions in which they live and the treatment that they receive do not cause any mental distress or suffering

These freedoms are all a very basic minimum for any animal, and if you are unable or unwilling to provide these for them, then you should really be questioning your suitability for dog ownership. However, I would hope that all of you that have found yourselves here are already providing these things subconsciously for your dogs, as they are based on simply showing kindness. Ensuring all of these outlines are met, will of course go some way towards your own dog feeling content, however this book will provide you with a more detailed outline of how to ensure your dog is the happiest they can possibly be, far exceeding the limits of these guidelines.

If you wish to know exactly how to achieve complete canine contentment with your own dog at home, then you have found yourself in the right place. This book will provide you with all the information and advice you require, to not only improve your relationship with your dog, but also how to enhance their lives to make sure that their happiness and wellbeing is continuous.

I understand all too well how owners are often frustrated by their dog's behaviour and the fact that they simply do not know how to remedy the issues they are facing, which is commonly due to a lack of understanding of what may be causing the issues in the first instance. The journeys that I have shared with my own current dogs, combined with working professionally with dogs for the past several years, have culminated in the advice and information I will share with you in here.

We will discuss many different aspects of dog ownership in turn and then discover how they all work harmoniously together in relation to your dog's happiness and contentment. Your dog's diet, the amount of exercise they receive, the training methods you use to teach them new skills, the enrichment activities they are provided with and the socialisation they experience, all play their own key roles in ensuring your dog's happiness. We shall also explore how being able to analyse your dog's body language effectively will help you to better understand their communication and finally discover the truth behind some common misconceptions and myths surrounding our dogs, with the aim of providing you with a clearer understanding of the dog you share your life with.

By increasing your understanding of your dog's exact needs through reading this book, I am positive that this will result in not only an improved, strengthened relationship between you, but also a calmer, happier and more contented dog overall too. Therefore, I would encourage you to read the book as a whole, as I am passionate in my belief that a more wholesome approach to canine behaviour, welfare and contentment, as opposed to focussing solely on an individual aspect in particular, creates better, longer lasting results.

Think of this as an adventure that you are sharing with your dog by your side, as you travel down this road of discovery together, and in the process, you will strengthen the bond you share with each other, and improve their lives along the way. Don't feel guilty if there are things you discover here that you have not previously considered, we are all on a constant learning journey, so we should always be open to new opportunities to further enhance our dog's life, based on the knowledge we currently have. Just the fact that you have purchased this book is the first step in the right direction and proves that you are already in the mindset of wanting to help your dog to be happier, which is amazing in itself!

Instead of feeling overwhelmed at the extent of the possible changes and additions you feel would benefit your dog, simply gradually add them in one by one and watch as your dog reaps the benefits. Achieving canine contentment is not a race; it is a lifelong project that you and your dog can actively work together on. It is not as straight forward as just working through each of the contents of the chapters here once and saying you have completed it, as there will be many different twists and turns on the road ahead of you, so be prepared to work hard to maintain your dog's happiness throughout their various life stages.

We must always be sure to remember, that we choose to bring a dog into our lives, and all too often we expect them to just slot into our routine, without properly considering their needs, which is where many behavioural issues can stem from. Unfortunately, in many circumstances, it is rarely as easy as simply choosing a dog, bringing them home and then living happily ever after. However, with the right guidance, information and kind methods, this can become much more of a reality than a fairy-tale. This is where 'Canine Contentment – The Essential Guide' steps in...

Enjoy!

Socialisation and Habituation

Socialisation - 'The process of training people or animals to behave in a way that others in the group think is suitable'

Habituation - 'The process of people or animals becoming used to something, so that they no longer find it unpleasant or think of it as a threat'

The main difference between socialisation and habituation is that socialisation is to do with your dog learning how to interpret the body language of other dogs and in turn how to behave appropriately around them. It also includes dog to human interactions and shows your dog how to behave appropriately around humans. Habituation is more to do with getting your dog used to every day sights, sounds and smells so that they learn not to be afraid of them or consider them to be threatening. Habituation is considered more temporary so it therefore requires consistent exposure to situations and encounters to ensure your dog continues to feel comfortable around them. During periods of prolonged absence from the exposure, your dog can regress and in turn begin to show fear to things when they are reintroduced.

For example, fireworks can be a common form of distress for a dog and because they only happen usually once a year, your dog does not have the opportunity to habituate to them, therefore they will likely get stressed every year. To overcome this, you may find it beneficial to play firework noises at a low level regularly and rewarding your dog for remaining calm, before gradually increasing the volume.

The same can be said for traffic, a young puppy may be walked near busy roads and habituated to the sights, sounds and smells of the traffic; they could then be rehomed to a quiet rural area, where they rarely encounter traffic. If they then encounter noisy traffic once again after a prolonged period of absence, it is likely they may be fearful or reactive towards it as they can no longer deal with it calmly. In cases such as this, the traffic should then be reintroduced gradually, so as not to overwhelm them and in turn prevent future behavioural issues surrounding the traffic from arising.

Socialisation begins from the moment a puppy is born, as they start their journey into our world. By spending time with their littermates, as well as with their mother, even before their eyes are opened, they begin to understand how other dogs behave. Once their needle-sharp puppy teeth first come through, they then begin to learn crucial lessons surrounding 'bite inhibition' as if they were to bite down too hard on their mother, they are likely to be reprimanded by her, which teaches them that this behaviour is not acceptable. This lesson is also backed up through them playing with their siblings, as if one puppy gets too rough and again bites or mouths a little too hard, then the other puppy is likely to yelp to signal that was painful. Problems can occur with puppies that are 'singletons' whereby they are the only puppy born, or the only surviving puppy in a litter, as well as with those that are removed from their littermates and mothers too soon. These puppies then do not have the opportunity to experience these lessons in bite inhibition effectively as they have nobody to teach them.

Humans can potentially teach their puppies bite inhibition through clear consistent guidance, but it is important to remember that even puppies who have learned this effectively, can sometimes slip up and bite, often because they are over tired and cannot make better choices.

Socialisation is easiest with puppies under 12 weeks of age, simply because they are more willing to approach new situations and encounters without fear, and after this point they do tend to become more cautious, but that is not to say that they cannot continue to be socialised with some kind and effective guidance. In an ideal world, a puppy's breeder should begin their socialisation process as early as possible, getting them used to interacting with other dogs, other animals and humans of all ages. This will give them a good head start compared to those who have not had any of these experiences from a young age.

For dogs that have missed the crucial early socialisation window, whilst it may be more difficult, all is not lost. Delta was incredibly ill as a puppy, in fact she was ill for the majority of her first six months of life, therefore she spent huge portions of her puppyhood, either in the vets, or recuperating at home. With all this in mind, she totally missed any chances of socialisation with the outside world, coupled with her being the only surviving puppy from her litter and her mother rejecting her, she really had a far from ideal start to life in socialisation terms. So, it has always been a very uphill struggle in order to not only try and socialise and habituate her effectively, but also with managing her fearfulness in order to socialise her with anything at all and she still struggles greatly with certain new encounters even now.

The main take away from Delta's story is that we must accept the dogs that we have, not the ones we think we should have. Just because my other three dogs are sociable as they were all well socialised from an early age, this does not mean that I should set the same high expectations for Delta, who quite frankly, is lucky to be alive at all.

She will never be a dog that I can take to a coffee shop, or one that would play with another dog in the park, but I am accepting of that and her life is enriched and happy without these things. For me to force her into situations such as these, just to satisfy my own ego, would not only be totally unfair but it also raises the question as to why I would be doing it?
Who would benefit from it? Me? Delta? Would she have a better life if she liked other dogs more? The short answer is that none of us would benefit, and it would have no positive impact on her life to cause her heightened levels of fear, stress and anxiety, every single day, just so she fits into a box that society has created for her, where she must always love everyone and everything she encounters and be permanently happy.

It is important to balance the need for effective socialisation with making sure your puppy's health is not being put at risk. Therefore, it is crucial that they are fully vaccinated before interacting with dogs with an unknown vaccination status, or visiting public spaces like parks. They can still be socialised with fully vaccinated dogs and trusted humans before their vaccinations are complete however, as it is hugely important that they have the chance to experience these interactions safely. As we will discuss in the Veterinary Care chapter, many vets now offer 'Puppy Parties' in which your puppy can socialise with other puppies of similar ages to them, in the safe, sterile environment of the veterinary practice, which drastically the reduces the risk of them coming into contact with harmful diseases before they are fully vaccinated against them. This allows the puppies to play with each other, and through this play they continue to learn what is acceptable and what isn't, with their interactions with others.

Where possible, the situations your puppy encounters should be engineered to be as positive as possible for them and anything too unpleasant should be avoided so as not to make them unwilling to experience new things in the future. Whilst their optimum socialisation window is relatively short, this is not an excuse to rush through everything all at once and totally overwhelm your puppy in the process as this can in fact be detrimental. Try to limit the number of new experiences and encounters your puppy has in a single day, taking care to remember that they need ample rest and relaxation opportunities in order to process new learning effectively. A group puppy training class using positive methods is always a good place to start, even if you feel you already have the skills required to train your puppy yourself at home as this setting allows your puppy to learn how to concentrate around the distractions of a class dynamic. It also provides an opportunity to learn appropriate interactions with other dogs of different shapes and sizes, as well as new people, which is something that cannot be easily replicated at home.

Whilst many puppy classes offer an opportunity at the end of the training session for the puppies to play, it is important to discourage overzealous play with other dogs, particularly larger ones as your puppy could get injured accidentally during the process. This advice applies in any setting where your puppy is playing or interacting with other dogs and you should also consider the body language of both dogs to ensure they are both happy for the play to continue. We shall look at body language in more detail in the dedicated chapter later on in the book. It is apparent that some well socialised adult dogs, have the ability to inhibit their own behaviours to make them more inviting and palatable to young puppies or inexperienced older dogs. For example, Inka naturally plays relatively roughly with other dogs, particularly when they are having a game of tug-of- war, however, if ever she encounters puppies, she adjusts her play style to suit them more. She becomes gentler, and does not pull the tug toy as hard as she would ordinarily, and she allows the puppy to 'win' the game regularly.

It is important to remember though that puppies get very easily tired and, in the process, they lose the ability to make good choices, which is why their behaviour tends to deteriorate. They may begin biting or mouthing more, or may persistently jump up or seemingly switch off from you completely. This is not because they are being naughty, it is most probably because they are tired and they would benefit from some rest.

Below is a list of suggestions which would be beneficial for your dog to encounter, whether this is as a puppy, or as an older dog;

- Walking with a lead attached to a collar or harness
- Getting into, out of and travelling in a vehicle
- Tolerating gentle physical handling and examination
- People wearing glasses or sunglasses or hats or hoods, all of which can be confusing for a dog which has never encountered these things before, as they partially obscure the humans

face

- People pushing pushchairs, or those in wheelchairs or mobility scooters, or those using other walking aids such as walking sticks, crutches, walking frames etc.
- People putting up and holding umbrellas
- Different textures including; grass, mud, concrete, sand, bark, carpets, tiles, wood floors paving stones, gravel etc.

All of the aforementioned suggestions fall more into the habituation category as there is the potential for your dog to react fearfully or negatively to these situations if they are not regularly exposed to them. Ensure to take small steps and celebrate the small successes, don't feel as though this is a process you need to rush through, all's that will do it put extra pressure on to your dog, who is likely to already be feeling some anxiety around these new experiences so be patient with them and give them plenty of encouragement and high value rewards.

You may also feel tempted to rush this important process if you have recently adopted an older dog and you do not know their full socialisation history. For example, a common misconception is that a dog 'just needs to get used to being around other dogs' so in order to achieve that, a well-intentioned, yet misinformed, owner may choose to send their dog to a day-care facility, or take them to a busy park where they will meet loads of new dogs and people all at once.

However, try to think of something in life you are afraid of and do your best to avoid, let's use spiders for this analogy. If you are genuinely afraid of spiders, and you do not know how to behave appropriately around them, if I was to put you in a confined space with hundreds of them all over the room and let them crawl over you, you would react in one of two ways. You would either scream, panic and get yourself totally worked up or sit quietly, very still, as you are simply too afraid to move. Now just because in the latter option, you may appear calm on the outside, because you are sitting still, chances are, your heart rate would still be elevated and your stress levels would be raised through the roof! This does not mean you are no longer afraid of the spiders, nor are you enjoying their company, you are essentially just paralysed with fear. This is how your dog is likely to feel if they have not previously been socialised or learned how to interact with and behave around other dogs or new people, then they suddenly find themselves surrounded by them. This is a process known as 'Flooding' or 'Immersive Therapy' which is extremely controversial and in reality, it is a likely recipe for disaster and can actually exacerbate the issue instead of remedying it. After all, dogs tend to approach new situations with trepidation and simply forcing them to face their fears head on is usually detrimental. As previously mentioned, if I were to put Delta in that situation, I can guarantee she would feel she had no other option other than to escalate to biting one of the other dogs or the people, as she would have nowhere else to go, which is exactly what we want to avoid.

Exercise

Ensuring your dog has the correct amount of exercise is a key factor to their contentment, however, there is much more to it than just your stereotypical 'walk round the block.' We shall not only explore the importance of physical exercise, but also look into possible ways to make your dog's exercise more enjoyable for both of you. Imagine if your dog could be tired out from you actually walking them less, instead of more?

Firstly, there is a great deal of social pressure to fit into the expected 'norm' of walking your dog, for an hour at a time, twice a day, in all weathers, without fail. Now, if that is a viable option for you, then great, get out there and do it! However, there are likely to be many more suitable and enjoyable options available to you, some of which you may not have previously considered.

Sniffing

One of the most important things to consider is allowing your dog to sniff and explore on walks. As we will go on to look at in the Enrichment Chapter, sniffing is possibly the most important thing for any dog to be able to do. All too often, you see a dog being pulled along by their owners, when all's that they really want to do, is sniff the lamp post and investigate their surroundings. Just as many of us check social media, or read emails, or receive letters, sniffing is our dog's way of interacting with their environment, so they should not be denied the opportunity to practice this behaviour as regularly as possible. Walks that allow for ample sniffing opportunities are affectionately known as 'Sniffari's' and they most commonly let your dog choose their own route, simply by following their nose.

Particularly for those of us with high energy dogs or working breeds, it is important that we do not fall into the trap of continually increasing your dog's exercise levels more and more in order to tire them out. This is actually likely to have the opposite effect and instead of making your dog calmer, they will likely appear more highly strung and excessively energetic due to them constantly having high levels of adrenaline running through their body. Bearing this in mind, it is also strongly advisable to limit repetitive chase games such as using a 'ball launcher' to throw a tennis ball. Whilst this activity is undoubtedly enjoyable for some dogs, the adrenaline that is released during high intensity exercise such as this, makes it almost physically impossible for your dog to actually choose to stop chasing the ball, even when they are physically exhausted. Obsessive chase games such as this may also increase the risk of your dog developing injuries such as RSI (Repetitive Strain Injuries), ligament damage, particularly to the cruciate ligament found in the back legs or even chronic joint damage if it is regularly practiced over long periods of time. Whilst playing fetch is a favourite past time for many of our dogs, these sessions should be kept short, allowing plenty of time to recover in-between running to avoid exhaustion, as well as taking care to discourage excessive sliding, high jumping and potential bad landings and sudden stopping or changes of direction, all of which have the potential to easily cause injuries.

Off Lead Exercise

It is also hugely important to allow your dog some off lead exercise, so they can explore the world at their own pace, run freely and practice natural canine behaviours. If your dog does not have a good recall, you may wish to consider the use of a secure field, which can usually be hired out by the hour, allowing you to let your dog off the lead, safe in the knowledge that they cannot escape or come to any harm. Recall is one of the most important things you can teach your dog, not only so that they can participate in some off-lead fun, but also for their own safety above everything else and we will discuss how you can teach a reliable recall in the Positive Reinforcement Training chapter. It should be noted that unless you can guarantee that your dog will come back to you when you call them, then they should not be off lead in areas where they are likely to encounter other walkers or dogs, because not every person or dog will be comfortable with an off-lead dog, bounding up to them unannounced. However, no dog, regardless of their breed or recall ability, should be off lead around livestock of any kinds, both for their sakes and the welfare of the other animals. Livestock such as sheep and cows can be easily scared by unknown dogs, particularly if they are chased by them and it is likely to cause them great deals of emotional stress or even injuries in some cases. The stress of being chased by a dog has the potential to cause pregnant sheep to abort their lambs or they may well be injured in their attempts to escape from the dog. Not only this, but many have been mauled by dogs, often sustaining horrific injuries in the process which commonly prove fatal. Livestock also have the potential to injure your dog too, especially if they are a smaller breed, so it really is imperative for the safety and wellbeing of our dogs and the livestock, that situations such as this do not arise.

Play

Play is a natural behaviour for dogs to exhibit, whether that be playing with other dogs, or with humans, so it is important to allow your dog to express this need. However, not all dogs want to play with other dogs all of the time, for a whole host of reasons. They may have had a negative experience such as them being attacked by another dog, or they may be recovering from an illness or injury so perhaps they are in pain, or they may be older and suffering from decreased vision and hearing so their tolerance levels are lower. Do not force your dog to constantly seek the interaction of others, some dogs simply just prefer the company of humans to other dogs. That said, if you do have a dog that loves to play with others of their own kind and you find another dog who is happy to engage in play, then make sure that the play session does not get too over the top, and that both dogs are always enjoying the experience. If there is any sign of tension, stress or them feeling uncomfortable in any way, then the play should be ended and the dogs separated. We shall look at how to analyse body language in more detail in the Body Language chapter.

Social Etiquette

There are some unwritten rules when it comes to social etiquette when you are out walking your dog. It is considered good etiquette to put your dog on a lead, if another on lead dog is approaching, as you never know if that particular dog wants to interact with other dogs. They may be unsociable around other dogs, or they could be recovering from illness or injury so would not appreciate another dog potentially jumping on them or invading their personal space. It is also good manners to ask the other dog's owners if your dog is allowed to say hello to their dog and in doing so this will reduce the risk of any negative interactions occurring. Whilst there are strategies in place to let other dog walkers know from a distance if your dog is happy to be approached, the awareness if often not commonplace amongst all owners, or the equipment requires you to already be relatively close to the dog wearing it, in order to establish it's meaning which can limit the effectiveness of them. These commonly consist of dog collars, leads and coats of different colours all with different meanings, so if you see a dog with a yellow coat on which says 'Nervous' or 'I Need Space' then try to be respectful of that and give them plenty of space. Likewise, green collars and leads tend to signal that a dog is friendly whereas red usually means 'no dogs or do not approach.' If awareness of initiatives such as this one was more widespread, it has the potential to be very beneficial; however, as a matter of politeness and respect, you should always aim to give other dogs plenty of space, and to ask owner permission before letting your dog interact with theirs.

Once you are able to readily recognise canine body language, this will then enable you to much more effectively judge your dog's interactions with other dogs and people and know when to potentially intervene to stop a situation escalating into something more negative. For example, if your

dog meets another dog whilst they are both on lead, they quite commonly are forced to meet each other nose to nose, which is actually a very unnatural way for dogs to greet each other. Although us humans may find this behaviour unsavoury, dogs would always choose to greet each other by sniffing each other's bottoms instead of meeting face to face. As a rule of thumb, try to limit your dog's greetings to just a few seconds at a time, as tensions can soon build rapidly and you want to try and avoid any confrontation. This is particularly important when both dogs are on lead, as this is often when most confrontation occurs due to the dogs being less able to move themselves away from an interaction as easily as if they were off lead.

Walks don't just have to be on lead or off lead; you can incorporate other activities to keep it fun and engaging for your dog. Some suggestions could include:

Parkour – Although not quite as extreme as some of the human versions of parkour, where people free run up the side of buildings, it is easy to introduce some of the techniques into your dog's walks. It encourages owners to utilise the environment around them to add some fun to their dog's walks. Examples would include, encouraging your dogs to climb on top of fallen trees, or to walk across a bench, or to put their paws up onto a rock or to paddle through a river. Anything in your surrounding environment can potentially be useful to you, not only does it make things more enriching and fun for your dog, it will also increase their confidence and strengthen their relationship with you. Anything that your dog is not comfortable doing, should not be forced however, remember it should be enjoyable for them after all.

Outdoor Training – Practicing your training outdoors is a great way to really cement your dog's understanding of each behaviour. It is most commonly known as 'proofing' a behaviour, where it is practiced in many different areas without and with distractions. For example, if you only ever ask your dog to 'Sit' in your living room, on the rug, it is likely that they will associate the rug and that room as part of this behaviour. To combat this, you should ask your dog to exhibit this behaviour in many different situations and settings, which is where outdoor training is really useful. There are many more distractions outside; new scents, wild animals, other dogs, people, cyclists, horse-riders, traffic to name a few, so when you practice training there, your rewards should be increased and your expectations should be lower. Remember to set them up for success, not failure!

Hide & Seek – Hide and seek can be another way to keep your walks interesting. Hiding toys or treats in longer grass, around trees, in fallen logs or in shallow water for example adds another exciting element to your dog's walk whether they are on or off lead. You could also physically play hide and seek with your dog. This is easier if there are two people on the walk, one to distract or hold the dog, whilst the second person hides, however it can be done alone too. If your dog exhibits any signs of distress or anxiety, stop the game and return to them.

Changing Routes – Walking the same route on every walk can quickly become disinteresting for both you and your dog so it may be beneficial for you both to mix things up a bit. Go on an adventure or try somewhere new, which will be full of new sights and smells which will be good for both of you. Even changing the time of day that you walk will provide your dog the opportunity to experience new smells and sights than they would if you walked at the same time every day.

Dog Sports – There are many different types of dog sports that your dog can take part in, whether that is just for fun, or competitively, including; flyball, agility, cani-cross, obedience, field trials, dock-diving, heelwork to music, rally-obedience, livestock herding and many more. Whilst these are all forms of training too, they also contribute to your dog's physical exercise amounts. Research local dog training clubs in your area as many of them will offer taster sessions and can advise you the best way to get started in that chosen sport.

Exercise Amounts

Exercise amounts should always be appropriate for your dog's age, breed and health requirements. For example, young puppies should not be over-exercised as their skeletal systems, and muscles and growth plates are still forming and growing. The growth plates are areas of developing cartilage and bone, found at each end of the bones of a puppy's skeleton, which allow the bones to lengthen over time as a puppy grows and finishes puberty. Whilst these growth plates are still 'open' they can be prone to injury or damage so care must be taken to avoid such occurrences. Giving young puppies too much exercise over prolonged periods of time can be extremely detrimental to them in later life, so just because they could go on a daily 4 hour walk over uneven, rough terrain at 12 weeks old, does not mean that they should. Different breeds mature physically at different ages, with toy and smaller breeds tending to mature earlier than larger or giant breeds. Equally, as our dogs become more senior in age, you may find that they require reduced amounts if physical exercise as their stamina will be naturally declining and they may be experiencing joint or mobility issues. That is not to say however, that older dogs no longer require any exercise at all, in fact, it is often beneficial to keep them moving gently to maintain both their physical and mental health.

Daycare and Dog Walkers

Although I am sure we would all love to stay at home with our dogs all day, in reality, many of us have to go to work or have commitments meaning we are not always able to provide our dogs with enough exercise on our own. This is where dog walkers or daycare services prove to be increasingly popular. However, as the canine care world is widely unregulated, care must be taken to ensure that your dog walker or daycare provider, really are the most suitable people to care for your dog in your absence. All too often I see local dog walkers pull up to a field and let out up to 10 off lead dogs from their vehicle, who then run rampage over the field, disturbing other dogs and people who were previously enjoying a quiet walk. These dog walkers often have little to no control over the dogs, not only because of the sheer number of them, but also because they are all excessively excited and have so much pent-up energy, they would find it almost impossible to listen to verbal cues or guidance anyway. It is hugely advisable to meet your dog walker first and see what kind of areas they take their dogs to and how they interact with them, it is vital that they share the same kind methodology as you do, in order to maintain the good work you are putting in with your dog, and also to enable them to build trust between your dog and themselves. I hear many stories of how normally confident, friendly dogs are hiding under the kitchen table when the dog walker comes to collect them, which is very alarming as they should be forming positive associations with their dog walker coming to take them on an adventure, so they should therefore be pleased to see them, not trying to avoid them.

Looking after someone's dog is a huge responsibility, so this should not be taken lightly. Any reputable dog walker or day-care provider should be happy to answer any questions or queries you may have about the services they provide. Sadly, many dog walkers or day-care providers are fuelled only by the money to be made in the industry as opposed to having each individual dog's needs and welfare at the heart of how they care for them, hence why some are tempted to accept high numbers of dogs at any one time to make it more profitable. That said, there are of course many reputable, trustworthy dog care providers available, it is just a case of choosing one both you and your dog feel comfortable with, who are able to provide your dog with the exercise and mental stimulation they require, whilst being kind and patient with them.

Diet & Nutrition

Diet is not as straightforward as just feeding your dog the right amount of food each day, in fact, it plays a much bigger role in your dog's contentment than you may realise. In this chapter, we will explore how your dog's diet can impact their behaviour and in turn, their overall happiness.

If we look back even just 20 years, it was common place to feed your dog a plain mixer biscuit, topped off with a can of wet food and possibly some scraps from the human's dinner plates. Whilst many dogs fared well on a diet such as this, there is now much more information readily available on the pros and cons of different food options, allowing us to make more informed choices when it comes to our dog's diet.

There are many different options available today for the type of food to feed your dog, the most common one being a kibble-based product. Other options include raw food, wet food or even home-cooked meals. There is no right or wrong decision to be made here, but you should always consider your dog's age, breed, activity level or any health issues they may have, in order to make an informed decision that is best suited to their individual circumstances. It should also be noted that the most expensive option does not automatically mean that it is the highest quality food, nor does it mean that the food will be best suited to your dog. Careful research on your part, into the best food for your own dog will always be required and this may alter as your dog reaches different life stages, so be prepared to change foods if you find a better option for your current set of circumstances.

All dog food can be split into two categories, either Complete or Complementary. Complete foods are called so, because legally they must contain everything required for a dog to remain healthy, without the need to add anything to their diet.
Complementary foods are designed to be fed in addition to other foods as they do not contain all the necessary nutrients required to feed these solely. Here, we will explore the various different available options in a little more detail:

Kibble

Dry Extruded – This is the most commonly used kibble variety, and it is available to purchase pretty much anywhere now, including pet stores, supermarkets and usually even in small local convenience shops. It has no specialised storage requirements and does not require any specific preparation aside from scooping the desired amount into your dog's bowl, hence why it is so popular with dog owners.

Dry extruded food is produced by passing ground, pre-mixed, dry ingredients through an industrial steam cooker, before being cut into the individual kibble pieces we are used to seeing as our dog's food. These kibble pieces are then quickly dried in very high temperatures, cooled and then usually coated to improve their flavour and palatability to our dogs.

Whilst fans of this commonplace diet argue that the cooking process ensures that any potential parasites will be killed, some are now concerned that these high temperatures may in fact destroy some of the nutrients found in the ingredients in the process.

Baking – Baked kibble starts life in a similar way to the dry extruded varieties, however the cooking process is different here. As the name suggests, the kibble is baked slowly in industrial ovens which is thought to better maintain the nutrient levels. However, the detriment to this option, is that they often need to contain higher levels of wheat and gluten in order to hold the biscuits shape, which can be a downside, particularly for dogs with intolerances or allergies.

Cold Pressed – In comparison to the two previous options, cold pressed diets are relatively new to the market. Again, they tend to start life as ground, pre-mixed ingredients, however instead of being cooked at high temperatures, they are as the name suggests, cold pressed. Some of the dried ground ingredients do need to be cooked still however, but the process is much less intensive.

Mixers – These fall into the Complementary category, so therefore they must be fed alongside other complete products such as wet food, raw food or complete kibble. They tend to be cereal based plain biscuits but some do occasionally have added vegetables and herbs included in them.

Air Dried - With air-dried products, the ingredients tend to start off fresh as opposed to dried and ground. The food is then gently heated to remove moisture via evaporation. This process reduces the damage to nutrients in comparison to the more traditional manufacturing methods mentioned above. Air dried food often needs to have water added to them before feeding in order to rehydrate them.

Freeze Dried – Similarly to air dried products, the ingredients tend to start off fresh as opposed to dried and ground. The ingredients are then frozen before being gently heated in a vacuum to remove moisture. By following this process, the nutrients are left almost totally intact within the food, meaning this is considered one of the most natural versions of dry food available on the market today. In the same way as air dried foods, freeze dried products also may need to be rehydrated before feeding by adding water to them.

Raw

Raw food has grown in popularity hugely over the past few years as it is regarded as the most natural way in which to feed your dog. It spans back for centuries, and it is what our ancestors would have fed their dogs when they first started cohabiting alongside humans. It is not without controversy though, and some critics question the safety of handling and feeding raw meats to our dogs because of the risk of cross contamination and developing diseases such as Salmonella. Any manufacturer of raw dog food, should be registered with DEFRA and measures should be taken to ensure that it is handled correctly.

Complete – Many companies are now producing complete raw food diets, which tend to be in the form of frozen minces, blocks or nugget pieces, which provide all the nutrients a dog requires to remain healthy, without the need to add anything extra to their diet.

DIY – This is how the raw feeding option really began. Owners created their own raw food diet for their dogs, taking into consideration the ratios of meat to bone content. This should only be done if you are confident that your knowledge will mean that your dog truly is getting the correct levels of nutrition from their diet. Doing this incorrectly over extended periods of time is likely to be very detrimental to your dog's health and wellbeing.

Complementary – Complementary raw foods come in the form of things such as chicken wings, turkey necks or knuckle bones. These can be purchased frozen from pet stores or fresh from butchers or abattoirs. It is important to remember that they should not make up your dog's entire diet; they are to supplement a complete meal of some kind.

Wet Food

Whilst wet foods are not currently as widely purchased as they once were, they are still a popular option for many dog owners today. The ingredients are mixed, cooked and then vacuum sealed into containers, before being heat sterilised to ensure a lengthy shelf life. Most commonly they come in tins, pouches or trays. Similar to the kibble options, some are concerned that the cooking and sterilisation process at high temperatures may remove nutrients from the final product.

Because, as the name suggests, wet foods contain much higher water content than kibble equivalents, you are required to feed it in higher quantities. However, this can be beneficial for dogs who naturally do not drink very much water or for those prone to urinary issues.

Fresh Food

Another relatively new option to the market, complete fresh foods can be purchased most commonly in trays or pouches. They mimic home cooked meals, so they often use higher quality ingredients than traditional complete wet or dry foods and are likely to retain higher levels of nutrients as processing is kept to a minimum. However, their shelf life is usually as little as 12-14 days from manufacture, which is clearly a lot less than the aforementioned options. They must be kept refrigerated, even before they are opened, or they can be frozen and defrosted before feeding, as and when required.

Home Cooked

This is a fairly uncommon option for many dog owners, as it is relatively labour intensive and time-consuming process. Some owners may choose this method for short periods of time, for example when their dogs are recovering from illness or surgery, they may choose to cook their dog's meals at home.

Prescription

There may be occasions where prescription diets are the only thing that is suitable for your dog. For example, they may be recovering from an illness or surgical operation, or they may have a long-term chronic health condition, which is managed through their diet as well as medication. These should only be fed under supervision from your vet as they often contain very specific nutrients to assist with certain health concerns, which can be detrimental to a healthy dog's wellbeing long term, if they do not require them. For example, dogs with Kidney Disease would be recommended to eat a diet low in Phosphorous, which would be unsuitable to feed to a dog without Kidney Disease long term.

Treats

Diet is not just what your dog eats as part of their meals; it also includes any other food they get over the course of the day, including treats! A common oversight an owner may face when their dogs are overweight, is them being unable to understand 'why is my dog not losing weight?' 'They only have this portion of food per day' but what they fail to factor in is the amount of treats their dog is consuming. The crust from our sandwich, the treats we use to train them, the chew they get to clean their teeth, the last snack before bed and the biscuit they had just for being super cute all contain calories after all!

However, treats can be an important part of your dog's wellbeing. Longer lasting chews or even puzzle toys are a great way to encourage your dogs to relax and de-stress. Chewing is a natural stress reliever for dogs so it is hugely important to allow them to practice this regularly. Just be sure to reduce the amount of your dog's main meals in relation to how many treats they get to avoid any unwanted weight gain.

Foods to Avoid

There are also many foods that can actually be toxic if your dog was to consume them. These include; chocolate, raisins/sultanas/currants, grapes, macadamia nuts, caffeine, alcohol and Xylitol which is a man-made sweetener which is often found in 'sugar-free' products. As our dogs may not inherently know what foods to avoid, it is our responsibility as owners to make sure that anything potentially dangerous to their health is always kept well away from them.

Where possible, highly processed foods which are high in sugar or fat should also be avoided and this goes for treats too! Foods and treats such as these are likely to cause your dog to appear 'hyperactive' which increases the risk of you as their owner, feeling frustrated or overwhelmed at their behaviour. This is similar to the old adage of 'giving children blue Smarties' as they were previously so full of sugar, additives and colourings, they often had a detrimental effect on a child's behaviour. If you are stressed and constantly telling your dog off or asking them not to do things, when they simply have too much energy that they do not know what to do with, then it is likely that your dog will feel stressed too. Equally, dogs that are not getting the correct levels of nutrition that they require may be lethargic or disinterested and reluctant to engage in everyday activities. Long term, this is also likely to increase their risk of developing illnesses too.

There has been a recent increase in alternative diets becoming available for your dog, which are more in line with human needs than those of your dog. We must remember that our dog's are omnivores so their digestive systems are designed to digest both meat and plants so for us to provide them with a vegetarian or vegan diet because of our own beliefs would not only be inappropriate, but actually likely to be harmful to them long term.

Hydration

Ensure your dog always has access to fresh, clean water at all times. You may notice your dog drinks more or less water dependent on their diet, so make note of how much is a normal amount for your dog. If they suddenly begin to drink more water than they normally do, it is best to arrange a veterinary check to rule out any underlying health issues.

There are now many other forms of 'dog suitable drinks' on the market including puppy and dog milks and even alcohol style drinks, however I would question the necessity of providing these for your dog on a regular basis as they are often full of preservatives, sugar and colourings which is not something that should be encouraged. All your dog needs to remain hydrated is a constant supply of fresh, clean drinking water.

Meal Frequency

Consider splitting your dog's meals into at least two per day, as opposed to just one larger meal daily, as this will make it easier for them to digest and spread their energy reserves over the whole day. It may also reduce the risk of them developing GDV (Gastric Dilation and Volvulus) also known as Bloat, which is a life-threatening condition in which the dogs stomach twists and fills with gas. This then presses on other internal organs including the lungs, making it difficult for your dog to breathe and for enough blood to be pumped around the body. Whilst the stomach is twisted, it's blood supply will also be drastically reduced or even cut off completely, meaning the stomach itself may begin to die off. This is an urgent medical emergency and veterinary treatment should be sought as soon as possible if your dog shows any of the following symptoms; laboured or heavy breathing, a swollen or distended abdomen, excessive drooling or attempting to vomit unsuccessfully.

Weight Management

Diet also links into your dog's bodyweight; it is important to maintain a healthy body weight to keep them in optimal condition. They should not be allowed to become overweight as this will put extra stress on their joints, heart and other internal organs. Many dogs will simply keep eating, even if they are not actually hungry, so it is up to us to monitor their consumption carefully to maintain optimum health. Equally, being underweight is also detrimental to their health. If you adopt an underweight dog, it may be tempting to 'feed them up' but doing so can cause them more harm than good. This instead, should be done over a longer, controlled period of time and under the supervision of your vet to avoid any complications.

Feeding Positions

Another factor worth noting is the height and positioning of the bowl that your dog is eating from, especially for those of us with older dogs or those with mobility issues. It is likely that a larger dog or those with arthritis for example, may find it more comfortable to eat from a raised bowl, so that they do not have to bend down for extended periods of time. Or, those of us with Brachycephalic (flat faced) breeds like Pugs or Shih Tzu's may find it beneficial to fed them in a shallow bowl, to ensure they can reach their food more easily. If your dog is the kind to inhale their food faster than you can even put the bowl down, then it may be worth investing in a 'slow feeder bowl' or a food toy in order to slow them down a little. Slow feeder bowls often have rigid sections built into the bowl, or they are shaped into maze like channels, to make it more difficult for them to just gobble their food down as quickly as possible. Bowls such as this can be used with any kind of diet, dry, wet, raw etc. If your dog is fed kibble, there are also many different toys which can be filled with kibble which encourage your dog to move them around, and in the process kibble pieces are released from them. Slow feeders and food toys are also types of enrichment, as they engage your dog's brain too. We shall look at enrichment further in the next chapter.

Enrichment

The Oxford dictionary definition of enrichment is; 'The action of improving or enhancing the quality or value of something.'

In the dog world, this term refers to enriching a dog's environment, in order to encourage them to utilise their senses and provide an outlet for them to display natural canine behaviours such as chewing, licking, sniffing, digging and chasing. In doing so, this will release feel-good hormones known as endorphins, which makes a dog happier and more content, which is exactly what we want to achieve!

Enrichment is making huge headway in the dog world currently, as it is easily accessible to any dog, at any life stage, so it really is more straight forward than you may think to introduce it to your dog's life. Dogs that do not have a suitable outlet to channel their natural canine behaviours are likely to exhibit numerous behavioural issues including; unwanted chewing of furniture and possessions, digging up the garden or floorings in the home, separation anxiety or excessive barking to name but a few. All of these undesirable behaviours are usually apparent due to high levels of stress, excessive amount of energy and a build-up of frustration, all of which enrichment can help to combat.

Enrichment can also be particularly beneficial for dogs whose physical exercise amounts need to be reduced, whether that is temporarily or long term. For example, when Delta was spayed, she was around 18 months old and being a young Border Collie, she was understandably full of energy! The thought of not physically exercising a young, high energy breed like her for around two weeks post operatively, would fill many with utter dread, however, using a combination of enrichment techniques from our repertoire, it made both our lives a whole lot easier. Not only did her give her brain a great deal of mental stimulation, it also further strengthened our bond, as we treated it as an adventure of finding out what new things we could try out today. Your dog would understandably have raised stress levels following surgery, as they will most probably have a change in routine (not going for walks when they usually would, or staying on a lead when they are usually let off lead etc.) but it is also likely that they will have some level of pain at the surgery site and they may also have to contend with wearing protective equipment such as a plastic cone collar, an inflatable collar or a body suit to stop them being able to interfere with their wound until it is fully healed. The combination of all of these factors is undoubtedly going to increase their stress levels, which is also a great reason to introduce them to some enrichment activities during periods of convalescence.

As previously mentioned in the Exercise Chapter, sniffing is one of the most universally necessary behaviours for dogs to display, regardless of their breed or age. A dog's nose has up to 300 million scent receptors in them, compared to humans who only have around 6 million. The Olfactory Bulb located in the dog's brain is responsible for processing scent, and theirs are up to 40 times larger than that of a human brain! On average, $1/8^{th}$ of a dog's brain is dedicated solely to scent so that really does show how vitally important it is to them. Many enrichment techniques utilise your dogs innate desire to explore through sniffing and scents which is often why they find it so enjoyable.

There is often social pressure to simply keep increasing your dog's physical exercise levels in order to wear them out. However, what this is actually likely to do is increase your dog's stamina and in turn create a little mini athlete whose need for intense exercise cannot be satisfied. Whilst physical exercise is undoubtedly important to your dog's health and wellbeing, exercising their minds is also crucially important, yet it is often overlooked. This is where enrichment ideas are highly beneficial. Below we shall look at some of the enrichment options that are currently available to purchase or make yourself at home;

Shop Bought Equipment

There are extensive ranges of enrichment products now available in physical pet stores as well as through online retailers. Below are some of the most popular suggestions;

Puzzle Toys - There are several leading brands of puzzle toys, but they are becoming increasingly more widely available. Most commonly they involve hiding small pieces of food within the puzzle and your dog then has to figure out how to access them. It is important to start off at an easy level to introduce your dog to puzzle toys so that you are setting them up to succeed. If the puzzle is too difficult, it is likely to increase their frustration levels and cause them to lose interest which is something we want to avoid.

Food Toys – The most common form of food toy would be a ball in which you place kibble pieces, your dog should then be encouraged to move the ball around, in turn releasing the kibble pieces. This then acts as a reward and incentive for them to continue to play with the ball. There are also rubber toys which can be filled with wet food, or meat pastes which your dog has to lick and chew on in order to access their treats. Once your dog has got the hang of it, these filled food toys could even be frozen so that it increases the difficulty level by it taking them longer to access the food.

Interactive Toys – There are many toys which emit different sounds such as squeaks or honks, or they crinkle when they are chewed. Some are even battery operated and they play music or interesting noises when they are moved around. If your dog likes to play ball, consider getting a different shaped one so that when it bounces, it goes in different directions, to keep things interesting. Toys that comprise of multiple textures are also good for enrichment, as the different parts feel different when your dog holds or chews them.

Tug Toys – These are not only a good enrichment tool, but they can also strengthen your relationship with your dog through play. Chasing, grabbing and playing tug-of-war with a toy is highly enriching, however, it is also extremely exciting for your dog, so you would benefit from following these sessions up with a calmer activity.

Lick Mats – Relatively new to the market, lick mats are usually silicone type mats which contain different raised designs on them. These are then smothered in wet food, raw food, meat pastes etc. and your dog is encouraged to lick the contents off of the mat. The different textures are interesting for your dog and because they are getting a food reward, it is reinforcing for them to do repeat the process. These can also double as useful training aid, as they can be placed at the side of a bath when your dog is being washed, or on the wall when they are being groomed for example, to create a positive experience for them.

Snuffle Mats – These are most commonly backed with rubber matting to avoid the mat slipping, and fleece or other material is then threaded through mat to create interesting textures. Food can then be scattered and hidden within the fabric, and your dog is encouraged to snuffle and sniff out the treats. These are an example of a 'foraging' toy which encourages your dog to utilise their intricate sense of smell which is one of the most crucial natural behaviours they need to have a chance to exhibit regularly.

Ball Pool – A children's plastic paddling pool can make a great enrichment game for your dog, especially when you fill it with plastic play balls. Many dogs will enjoy diving in to retrieve a toy, or snuffling around to find scattered treats amongst the balls. Doing this will also increase their confidence, so if they are reluctant to go in at first, don't be tempted to pick them up and put them in or force them to, they will go in when they are ready. A ball pool can also double up as paddling pool on warmer days, which will not only help your dog to cool down, but it will also provide them with some much-needed mental stimulation if it is too hot to take them for a walk. You could add extra interest by adding toys that sink, as well as ones that float to encourage your dog to search for them.

Cuddly Toys – These are a real favourite of my dogs and so I often purchase teddies from charity shops for them to play with. Care should be taken to remove any hard plastic eyes or noses from the teddies, as they can be a danger to your dog if they swallow them. It is also advisable to avoid those with 'beans' in them as a stuffing material, as again they can easily be ingested accidentally. So many people say 'I won't give my dogs cuddly toys because all's they do is rip them up' but I would argue that that is actually all part of the fun! Just be prepared to be picking up bits of stuffing afterwards and as with any toy, you should supervise your dog whilst they are playing with them and remove them when they are damaged.

Play - Play is a vital part of your dog's happiness and although there are thousands of products available, all with a specific aim in mind, sometimes it is nice for your dog to just simply play for playing sake. Whether that be them playing with other dogs, with you as their owner, or even on their own. One of my own dogs, Inka, can regularly be found just throwing a toy around on her own, or rolling in the grass outside, simply because she enjoys it and it makes her happy, so playtime does not always have to be structured for it to be enriching.

Home Made Equipment

There are also loads of home-made options for you to consider, which utilise things you may have already at home. The most common options include;

Cardboard Box – Most of us always seem to have a cardboard box lying around the house and these can be a great form of enrichment. Simply fill them with old newspaper or magazines then scatter in dry treats or kibble to encourage your dog to sniff them out. It doesn't matter if they rip the box, that is all part of the fun! Just be prepared to tidy up afterwards.

Toilet Roll Tubes – Collect your cardboard toilet roll, kitchen roll or wrapping paper tubes and again stuff them with newspaper and hide treats inside. If you have several, you could even arrange them inside the cardboard box to increase the difficulty level. Another suggestion could be threading these treat-filled tubes onto some string and tying it up at your dog's head level and encouraging them to push the tubes around to release the treats. This reduces their ability to use their feet to pin down the tube, making them rely on just using their mouth which is more taxing for them.

Wrapping Presents – Many dogs enjoy ripping open presents – I mean, who doesn't love presents? If they have been treated to a new toy, consider wrapping it up before you give it them and encourage them to open it. Treats can also be used in the 'present' similar to the 'pass the parcel' game where each layer of the parcel contains small amounts of treats and/or toys.

Plastic Bottles – Every house has an empty plastic bottle at some point, so you can use this as a make your own interactive food toy. Simply cut small holes all over the bottle, and fill with dried treats or kibble. Encourage your dog to move the bottle around so that the treats fall out to reward them. To begin with, make sure there are plenty of large holes so the treats fall out relatively easily, then the holes can be reduced in size and number as they get the hang of it, to increase the difficulty level.

Muffin Tray – Muffin trays can be a great enrichment tool as they can be filled with different textures and treats in each section. For example, scrunched newspaper in one, hay in another, fabric pieces in the third and so on all with treats hidden amongst them.

Tasting Platters – Another form of enrichment is allowing your dog to taste different foods that they may not have access to on a day-to-day basis. Suggestions of items to fill your platter with could be; fruits, vegetables (cooked and raw), meat paste, cooked meats, dehydrated treats, cheese spread. Anything goes really! As many different tastes and textures as possible is the aim here, though take care to avoid anything that may be unsuitable for your dog to consume.

Scatter Feeding – A simple enrichment idea is to scatter your dog's food or treats in the garden or yard, so they have to sniff out their snacks. Or hide a treat somewhere in the house and encourage them to find out. As with any enrichment activity, it is important to set your dog up for success, particularly when they are trying something new. The difficulty level can then be increased gradually once they have gained confidence in the task.

Toy Rotation – Many of us have loads of toys

for our dogs and they can't possibly play with them all at once. Consider rotating your dog's toy collection so some are kept to one side and then they are reintroduced in replacement of their current options. This keeps their interest levels high. You could also let your dog choose their own toys, for example give them a selection of 5 different toys to play with and have a fun game with whichever one they decide on.

Trick Training

Trick training not only gives your dog's brain a good workout; it is also likely to improve the relationship you share with them. Plus, who can say no to a dog who wants you to shake their paw in return for a biscuit? As with all training, when teaching your dog tricks, this should be done via positive reinforcement methods, in order to maintain your dog's happiness and increase their chance of learning them successfully. We shall look at positive reinforcement training methods in more detail later on in the book.

Think of your dog's breed, if you don't know already what they were originally bred for, then research it! If you have a crossbreed, research all the breeds that make up your dog so that you have a clear idea what their natural breed traits are likely to be. For example, a Border Collie has been bred for thousands of years in order to excel at herding livestock, so one of their natural breed traits would be herding, which is why you often see them running in circles in the park! Or a Dachshund which has been bred as a hunting dog for badgers or other burrowing mammals, they are required to dig down into burrows and so one of their breed traits is digging. If dogs with such strong breed traits do not have a way to channel them appropriately then this can be a recipe for disaster. A favourite phrase of mine is 'If you do not give your dog a job to do, then they will go self- employed and you may not like the job they choose' For example, a Border Collie may chase cars, or bikes and a Dachshund may dig up the garden! It is an unrealistic expectation for our dogs to simply 'set aside' these intrinsic needs just for our own human convenience.

Body Language

We bring dogs into our lives and expect them to adapt to our hectic lifestyles and to understand our confusing communication methods and they often make huge efforts in an attempt to communicate with us, which unfortunately is all too often missed. With that in mind, it is the least we can do to learn how to interpret their body language, so that we can go some way to understanding them too. Learning how your dog is trying to communicate with you will help you to better understand their needs and how they are feeling, in order to keep them happy and content.

There are several kinds of body language that you should aim to recognise, particularly with regards to your own dog, but also in other dogs too, in order to better understand what they are trying to tell us. These include posture, facial expressions, verbalisations and other body language. Although the exact body language will differ in each individual dog, there are some key points to look out for. There are no definitive rules to say that every dog with display the exact same body language to communicate how they are feeling. After all, there are hundreds of different kinds of dogs, that come in all shapes and sizes, so the body language displayed by a Whippet would be different to that shown by a Labrador, and different again to a Jack Russell and so on. Even though all four of my dogs are the same breed and they all share similarities, they all have their own unique portrayals of body language so it is important to consider what each individual dog is trying to communicate at a given time and not make assumptions. Therefore, the whole spectrum of the body language should be considered as opposed to just one aspect of it, in order to form a more appropriate overview of what the dog is trying to communicate. However, generally speaking, the information below is a good starting point on what to be aware of and it provides some pointers to look out for;

Tail Positioning

A common misconception is that dogs only wag their tail when they are happy, however, dependent on their tail positioning and the way in which they are wagging it, it can in fact mean very different things. For example, when a dog is moving their tail in large sweeping motions from side to side, then this can indicate they are happy, but if the tail is being held tucked underneath them and they are only slightly moving the very tip of the tail, this is more likely to mean they are feeling anxious or nervous of the situation they are in. As a general rule, the tail positions below act a guide to how your dog may be feeling, however they should always be considered alongside other dog body language in order for you to make an informed assessment;

Happy – Large sweeping motions side to side

Nervous – Tail tucked under the body, moving the very tip of the tail

Alert – Tail held high and stiff

Scared – Tail tucked tightly under the body

Complications can arise with breeds whose tail is naturally held high or curled over their backs, such as is seen in Akitas or Pugs, as other dogs can commonly misinterpret this body language to mean something else more offensive, when really the other dog is trying to be friendly or neutral towards them. This can also be said for dogs with docked tails, or those that are naturally born without tails such as Australian Shepherds, as this can also make it more difficult for others dogs to interpret their body language effectively.

There have also been studies whose results suggest that even the direction in which your dog wags their tail can mean different things. It has been shown that tails that are wagged more to the left suggests the dog feels slightly uncomfortable or anxious whereas tails wagged more to the right indicates the dog is feeling happy and relaxed. For example, you may notice that when your dog sees a person or dog who they love and enjoy the company of, then they will wag their tail more to the right, yet if they see a person who is excessively authoritative over them, they may wag more to the left.

Ear Positioning

How your dog holds their ears is very much breed dependent as naturally some dog's ears are pricked and upright such as with a West Highland Terrier (Westie), whereas some are droopy and hang below the head such as with a Bloodhound. So, with these differences in mind, it can be difficult to provide a broad description of what to look out for. Generally speaking though, dogs who have their ears pinned back flat to their head are likely to be feeling fearful, anxious or stressed and those with ears pricked up straight is usually indicative of them being engaged and interested in their environment. Although thankfully ear cropping is now illegal in the United Kingdom under The Animal Welfare Act, there are still dogs who live here who have been imported from abroad where the practice is still relatively common amongst breeds such as Dobermans, Great Danes and some Bull Breeds. Cropping is when part of a dog's external ear flaps, officially known as Pinnae, are cut and removed. This can also cause communicative complications between dogs as they no longer have a full range of movement in the ear meaning they are less likely to be able to communicate with them as effectively. It is also thought to reduce the clarity of the dogs hearing as well, which is a huge price for the dog to pay simply because humans want them to look a certain way.

Facial Expressions

Analysing your dog's facial expressions can also play an important role in you being able to recognise what they are trying to communicate about how they are feeling. Possibly the most easily recognisable facial expression would be when a dog bares their teeth which we tend to associate with aggression, however it can be a little more complex than it first seems. For example, if a dog is showing all of their teeth, lips pulled tightly back, coupled with their ears being pinned back to their head and them growling, it is safe to assume that they are not happy and that if the situation is not rapidly diffused, then they may feel as though they have no choice but to escalate their reactions to a bite. However, one of my dogs,

Tizzy, 'Smiles' on a daily basis, where she too bares all of her teeth and gums but this is not because she is about to bite or because she feels threatened, in her case she does it when she sees a tennis ball, which is her favourite thing in the whole world. This demonstrates how crucial it is to consider your dog's body language, as well as the situation they are in as a whole to truly understand how they are feeling.

Facial expressions can be difficult for some dogs to portray effectively simply due to their facial structures. Brachycephalic breeds, or those with short noses and flat faces, such as French Bulldogs, Pugs, British Bulldogs and Boxers, can struggle to be understood by other dogs as they cannot read their facial expressions as well as they can for dogs with longer noses. This coupled with the fact that many of these breeds have a tendency to suffer with breathing difficulties because of their anatomy, means that their breathing may be noisier, raspy or sniffly, which can also be misinterpreted by other dogs.

Eyes

They say that the eyes are 'the window to the soul' and that can be particularly apparent in our dog's case. When your dog's eyes are soft and relaxed, it is safe to assume that they too are feeling calm too, however if their eyes appear hard or they are staring then it can mean that they are feeling threatened by something and do not want to let it out of their sights. If your dog is feeling anxious or stressed, they may display the whites of their eyes which is commonly known as 'whale eye.' In this situation, the dog may avert their head slightly, but their eyes will stay fixed on the thing causing them the distress. It is also worth noting that prolonged staring eye contact between dogs can indicate tensions are rising and to avoid the situation escalating to confrontation, the dogs should be separated.

Whilst pupil dilation is a natural occurrence dependent upon the amount of light in the dog's surroundings, it can also be an indicator of your dog's emotions. When your dog is in a dark environment, their pupils will dilate or enlarge to allow more light to enter the eye and when they are in a brighter environment, the pupils will constrict or get smaller, to reduce the amount of light entering the eye which is known as the pupillary response. However, their pupils may also dilate when they are feeling excited, aroused, nervous or stressed because in all of these situations, their inbuilt 'flight or fight' response is activated to either enhance their performance or keep them safe from harm. In such situations, your dog is required to analyse their surroundings quickly and effectively hence why their pupils will often dilate to allow them to do so.

Vocalisation

The most common types of vocalisations your dog may make would be barks, whines and growls, all of which can be further separated into more intricate divisions, all with their own meanings.

So, let's begin by looking at barking and what different sounding barks may mean;

Barking - High pitched repetitive barks may indicate excitement or frustration, for example when you are about to throw your dog's favourite toy and they simply cannot control their anticipation of what is about to happen.

A long howl, followed by a gap, followed by another howl can indicate loneliness, and it is most commonly seen in dogs suffering from separation anxiety from their owners whilst they are away from them.

Barking to indicate an alert, such as when your dog rushes to the door when somebody knocks, tend to be long strings of repetitive barks, with very short gaps between barks and suggest a sense of urgency. They also tend to be a lower pitch to essentially warn off the 'intruder.' The reason that dogs bark at the postman or delivery drivers is because in their minds, they bark and the postman leaves the house, so it has positively reinforced that their barking has been successful in achieving that. But we know that in reality, they are just carrying on with their deliveries. (But don't tell your dog!)

Growling - Some dogs growl a lot during play, but this does not automatically mean they are warning off their human or dog playmate, they may just be enjoying themselves. However, if the growl was a low, slow, belly growl, which was pared with staring eyes and stiff, still body language then it indicates something more sinister and the situation should be diffused to avoid any confrontation. Putting the growl into context should help you understand what your dog is trying to communicate so the whole scenario should be considered.

Whining - Whining can be indicative of many different emotions, but if the whine was to be paired with your dog pacing, trembling and being generally unsettled, then it is safe to assume they are feeling anxious or stressed. They may also whine for attention, which is why puppies often cry at night when you first bring them home as they are probably feeling lonely and overwhelmed.

Some dogs may also whine with excitement, in anticipation of them being about to receive their favourite tasty treat, their food, or their toy.

Taking the time to recognise and understand your own dogs often extensive vocalisations will help you better interpret what they are trying to communicate to you. Just like us humans, our dogs are all totally unique, so what may mean one thing for one dog, may mean something else for another one, making it imperative to consider the whole scenario.

Raised Hackles

Raised hackles on a dog is scientifically known as piloerection, and it is where the hairs on your dog's body stand on end, most commonly from the base of the neck and down the spine. It is similar to 'goose bumps' in humans and it is an involuntary response from the dog's nervous system, meaning it occurs naturally and automatically beyond your dog's control. Most commonly, it is associated with aggression, as the dog is seen to be trying to make themselves look bigger; however it is actually more to do with arousal levels which can be raised due to stress, anxiety, fear or excitement so it does not automatically mean that your dog is aggressive. Other factors such as body positioning and how they are holding their ears and tail should be considered alongside the raised hackles to determine the reasoning behind them. For example, a dog meeting another nose to nose, who both have raised hackles, are standing still and tall, with pricked ears and a stiff tail are likely to be about to come to sort of disagreement. However, a dog that has just been startled by a sudden loud noise may also experience raised hackles as they are fearful and defensive, not because they are aggressive.

Appeasement

Appeasement gestures are non-confrontational body postures used by our dogs to communicate that they are not threatening and they come in peace. The main aim of dogs portraying these appeasement gestures is to avoid any confrontation between themselves and other dogs as well as between themselves and humans. A common example of a dog displaying appeasement behaviours would be when their owner returns home to find their dog has chewed on the dining table leg. Their owner says their dog looks 'guilty' because they have done something wrong but it is much more likely that the dog has picked up on their anger or anxiety and therefore offered an appeasement gesture, to diffuse the situation and avoid confrontation from their owner.

They most commonly look like this;

- Your dog rolls onto their back, showing their belly
- They may carry their body low down to the ground
- They may even urinate slightly
- More subtle signs include lip licking, yawning and averting their eyes or whole head.

These gestures can also be used in order to distract away from a situation your dog feels uncomfortable or stressed in, which is known as 'Displacement Behaviours.' An example of displacement being used would be when a dog is called back by an owner who uses forceful or harsh training methods, meaning the dog is reluctant to return to them through fear, so they may begin sniffing, or scratching themselves in order to delay their return.

Whilst appeasement gestures and displacement behaviours are often more subtle, you should take great care to learn them and act upon them, as they are often the first signs that your dog is uncomfortable with the situation, and being able to recognise their anxiety at this early stage, will prevent the situation escalating further.

Human Body Language

We should also take care to notice our own body language when we are in the company of our dogs. They often take notice of our every move, so they can predict what we are about to do next and react accordingly, therefore your body language is crucial. So much so, our dogs are sometimes that in tune to us, they respond to even the slightest change of body positioning or posture that to us can go totally unnoticed. For example, when we greet a new dog for the first time, many of us lean over the dog to go and stroke them straight away, when they may well have never seen us in their lives. In fact, dog owners and lovers can actually be the worst offenders for this, as they are naturally more comfortable around dogs, they then automatically assume that every dog will then be immediately comfortable around them as well which is not always the case. If you try and look at it from a dog's perspective, then there is a large figure looming over you, often making direct eye contact, reaching out a hand towards your face and over your head to stroke you, all of which could be considered confrontational. Another common misconception in this situation is reaching out your hand to let a new dog sniff you, which can in fact cause them more stress and anxiety as the hand movement may startle them.

Remember your dog's sense of smell is incredible, so they can smell you as soon as you start walking up the street towards them, so they certainly have nothing to gain from having your hand a few centimetres from their face. Instead, let the dog approach you in their own time, ideally standing side on to them and avoiding direct or staring eye contact and do not rush your encounter with them. By you understanding how to read a dog's body language, it will better enable you to act appropriately around them, as you can see exactly how they are feeling and what they are trying to communicate as a result of your body language around them.

Rest & Relaxation

Rest is a vital part of your dog's wellbeing, yet unfortunately, it is often very much overlooked in favour of increased amounts of physical exercise and mental stimulation.

Puppies particularly need much more rest than you would imagine, dependent on their age and breed, they can need up to 18 to 20 hours sleep per day! What is also important to remember here, is that puppies and younger dogs are much less able to 'self-settle' so even if they are really tired and need to rest, they will not actively choose to stop interaction or being involved in an activity, in order to sleep. Therefore, it would be beneficial to schedule rest and sleep times for your puppy, to ensure they are getting enough time to relax and rest. Sleep is a crucial part of your puppy's development, as only when they are fully asleep can they process any new learning or experiences that they have come across more effectively.

It is important to provide your dog with a comfortable resting place, which is consistently available to them. This can be their own dog bed, the sofa, the armchair, your bed, wherever you choose, provided that they always have access to it. Some dogs benefit from a den style resting place, which is where crates can be useful. There are also igloo style beds available on the market or you could create their own space to suit their needs. My eldest dog, Sky, has taken residence in the built-in- wardrobe, and chooses to take herself off there when she wants some time to herself. All dogs should always have access to somewhere quiet, where they will not be disturbed, so that they can decompress effectively. This is particularly important if your dog shares their home with other dogs, other family pets or babies and/or young children.

For those of us with high-energy, working breeds, there is often a large emphasis on exercising your dog's more and more in order to wear them out, however, this can in fact cause you to inadvertently create a canine athlete, that is super fit and in turn needs further increased levels of exercise.

Obviously, if you are in a position to maintain this long term, then great, however in reality this is not always a viable or even a healthy option. When a dog exercises, particularly if it is high intensity exercise such as repetitively chasing a ball, hormones known as Adrenaline and Cortisol are released. Adrenaline is released when your dog is feeling an extreme emotion, including excitement or stress and in turn it increases their heart rate, breathing rate and blood pressure.

Similarly, Cortisol is also released in these situations and that too causes similar physiological effects for your dog, but is more commonly linked to feelings of fear, stress or being threatened.

Because these hormones stay in your dog's system, long after their exercise is over, it may cause them to still appear on edge, or full of energy and it is also likely to cause your dog to continue running long after they are physically exhausted. This is where it is vitally important to encourage your dog to rest, as whilst they sleep, their Cortisol and Adrenaline levels begin to decrease back down to more normal levels. It is worth noting that Cortisol levels can stay in your dog's bloodstream for up to 72 hours, so ensure they have plenty of time to relax and decompress in between exciting or stressful experiences. This is particularly important for those of us with reactive dogs, that struggle to process the outside world as well as other dogs.

For example, Delta is reactive around other dogs and people that she does not know, and this manifests itself through her barking and lunging if they come too close to her. Although every effort is made to prevent her being put in a situation where she has no other choice but to behave in this way, there are still instances where it is unavoidable. When situations like this arise, it causes a huge influx of Adrenaline and Cortisol hormones to race through her body, as she feels threatened, often leaving her on edge for the remainder of her walk and long after we have returned home. With this in mind, we will then often decide to skip her walks for the next day or so, and choose to do enrichment activities at home with her instead, to help her decompress and give time for her Cortisol levels to reduce. If we simply carried on with a normal walking schedule, whilst her Cortisol levels were still very high, then it would mean we were setting her up for failure, instead of success. She would be much more likely to react negatively, even to situations that she would otherwise tolerate relatively well, simply because she is already feeling stressed. The suggestion of factoring rest days into your dog's routine, is often met with phrases such as 'there is no way I can't take my dog out for a walk all day, they will destroy the house' but I am not suggesting that your dog simply does nothing at all for the full day. Instead, consider some the enrichment activities we discussed in the 'Enrichment' chapter as this will not only provide them with some mental stimulation, but it will also give them time to decompress and relax too. Chewing is a huge stress reliever for our dogs, so providing them with an outlet to practice this appropriately, as opposed to them chewing up the television remote, would be very beneficial to help them relax.

When your dog is relaxed or sleeping, their Parasympathetic nervous system which is also known as the 'Rest and Digest' function can operate most effectively. This means that their heart rate is reduced, as too is their breathing rate to allow more energy to be channelled into their intestinal activity, meaning digestion is more effective during this time. This may be why dogs that appear to be in a constant state of stress or anxiety, suffer frequent bouts of diarrhoea, vomiting or being off their food, as all of their energy is being focussed on the Sympathetic nervous system. This system is responsible for instead directing their energy reserves to the limbs and brain so they are essentially ready to either flee the situation that is causing them stress or to help improve their performance should they need to confront something dangerous, most commonly known as the 'Flight or Fight' reaction.

When considering your dog's rest and relaxation times, it is also important to factor in your own stress levels and how much time you yourself factor into your day to unwind. As we all know, dogs are exceptionally in tune to our own human emotions, this is often a reason why we love them so much as they seem to care about us as much as we do about them. Therefore, if you are stressed, anxious or feeling highly strung, then this will undoubtedly be picked up by your dog as well. This may also result in your patience or tolerance levels being depleted, as you are already stressed which can mean that you snap at your dog or tell them off, when they are in reality, not doing anything wrong. Consider creating time in your day for short meditation sessions, this will help you be more present in the moment, calming you down and in turn, relaxing your dog in the process. Or practice some self-care exercises, such as having a warm bubble bath, indulging in your favourite biscuit with your afternoon cup of tea or listening to your favourite songs with no distractions, whatever makes you feel relaxed and calm. These suggestions are things that I personally have found to be beneficial to me, but you should tailor yours more appropriately to your own needs and feelings.

Along similar lines, your dog's often go through a process known as 'Trigger Stacking' which can also apply to us humans as well. Trigger Stacking is essentially lots of small potentially stressful, encounters or situations occurring over a period of time, until one thing pushes you to react negatively, 'the final straw,' so to speak. For example, when Delta has had ample opportunity to calm down and decompress, she tends to be able to deal with things more appropriately, as opposed to when she is already in a heightened state of stress or anxiousness. So, we could go for a walk and pass a man on the other side of the road, which does not elicit a reaction, then we could see another dog playing several hundred metres away on the other side of the field, then we could encounter a small child playing on the park swings, we could then play a game of fetch in the field before making our way back home. Then a cat could run across the road ahead of us, before we then see the same man who we saw at the start of our walk, only this time, Delta may bark at him defensively even though she showed no reaction to the exact same man just an hour or so previously. Think of each of these potential triggers as some liquid in a cup, each one tops up the cup a different amount, depending on the level of stress they create for our dog. Then gradually over time, the cup gets fuller and fuller until it overflows, and it is this overflow that represents the negative reaction Delta showed by barking. However, if there is ample opportunity for your dog to rest, relax and recover from being subjected to these triggers, then they are then less likely to react negatively as quickly, as their tolerance levels are increased again. Each dog will have a different sized theoretical 'cup' so some dogs may be able to effectively tolerate a whole host of different potential triggers with ease, whereas others will struggle more to do so.

The same can be said for us humans, I am sure you are familiar with the phrase 'there is no use crying over spilt milk' which is commonly used in reference to someone over reacting to a usually trivial situation. For example, if you spill your tea, if you are feeling calm, you would simply wipe it up and not give it a second thought. However, imagine you have missed your alarm, so you are now running late, in the process of getting ready, you drop toothpaste down your work clothes, forget to make your lunch, get stuck in traffic on the way to work and when you finally get chance to have a cup of tea on your break, you then spill it, causing you to overreact negatively. Again, each trigger fills up our proverbial cup bit by bit, until it will ultimately overflow, which is likely to cause you to overreact negatively to something you can normally deal with without an issue, exactly the same as our dogs can do. Like us, our dogs have good days and bad days, which further highlights the importance of allowing them plenty of time to rest and recover after stressful events.

Positive Reinforcement Training

Whilst this book is not designed to solely be a training manual, using appropriate, kind and effective training methods does play a crucial role in your dog's contentment. Knowing how to effectively communicate with and train your dog sets them up for success for living harmoniously alongside us. Here we shall look at the kindest way to teach your dog to do anything, known as positive reinforcement training.

Positive reinforcement basically means what it says on the tin, it is the act of rewarding a behaviour positively (through treats, toys or praise), in order to reinforce it and thereby increase the chance of the dog replicating that behaviour in the future. The reward should be chosen based on what is most motivating for your dog, which for many is food, but it can also be verbal praise or playing with a toy. Teaching your dog new things in this way, vastly increases the chance of your dog learning it successfully. The most common form of positive reinforcement training is known as 'Clicker Training' and this has been shown to have fantastic results when it is introduced and utilised correctly. It is the method I have used to teach all of my dogs everything they know to date, ranging from party tricks such as 'Play Dead' or 'High Five' to assisting with the reconditioning of more serious behaviour issues such as chasing cars or even the redirection of aggression.

If your dog has not previously experienced this method of training using a clicker, which is essentially a way of making an easily identifiable 'click' noise, then you need to go through a process known as 'Charging the Clicker' to begin with. What this means is that your dog needs to pair the click sound created by the clicker, with a high value reward, usually food, so every time they hear that click, they know that a tasty reward is incoming. To do so, simply click and give your dog a treat, then repeat this process for several repetitions, you may be surprised just how quickly your dog picks this up and begins to look to you for their reward once they hear the click. My high value rewards tend to consist of cooked meats, hotdog sausages or cheese most commonly, anything that your dog does not get as part of their normal diet, so that they are willing to try really hard to get hold of the rewards. These rewards only need to be tiny, and ideally, they need to be quick for your dog to eat, so as you do not lose valuable training time waiting for your dog to chew up larger treats and to also ensure that they don't fill up on treats and lose interest in training.

Remember that these treats all contain calories which should be factored into your dog's daily food allowance to avoid weight gain. Some trainers go as far as to say that you can use your dog's entire daily food allowance as food rewards, and get rid of meal times altogether, instead using their whole food allowance to train with throughout the day. Whilst this can be beneficial in some scenarios, I am not a huge believer in making your dog work for every single morsel of food they consume. I am sure I can speak for both you and I, when I say I would be unimpressed if I had to work hard and learn new behaviours constantly in order to get any food at all, sometimes it is nice for your dog (and for us!) to just enjoy a meal.

Before you start training, it may be useful for you to have a run through of your own training checklist, to make sure you have everything to hand before you begin, so as not to slow down any progress whilst you are searching for equipment or rewards. My training checklist looks something like this:

- Clicker

- High Value Treats
- High Value Toy

- Any equipment required for the particular trick we are working on. This could include a bell for 'Ring The Bell' or a mat for 'Wipe Your Paws' or your dog's toy box and toys for 'Tidy Up'
- Patience and positivity. These are the two most important things on your checklist and you will only succeed with your dog's training if you are kind, positive and patient with them whilst you navigate the world of training together.

Once your dog can effectively recognise that the click means a positive reward is on the way, then this is when training can properly begin. The main aim is for you to mark the exact moment that your dog shows a behaviour that is desirable for you, then to back that up with a positive reward.
This is also where you will likely realise that your timing is not as good as you thought (trust me, I have been there too!) but this is something you can work on, after all dog training is a two-way street and is a learning process for you and your dog together.

It is important to remember that training is not just something you do once, or for a short while when you first get your puppy or dog, it is a lifelong process and journey that you share with your dog. The aim of training should not be to create a dog which always behaves impeccably or almost robotically, but rather to help provide your dog with the ability to happily live alongside us in our often-confusing human world. In fact, a well-trained dog often has more freedom than one who has little to no training at all, simply because they can navigate the human world that they find themselves in, more successfully. I like to think of training as a language we share between ourselves and our dogs that we use to help one another understand what the other is asking of them.

Seeing as we are not dogs, and our dogs are not humans, we do not automatically have a shared language that we can both understand; therefore, we must create our own. This is where positive reinforcement training is really beneficial, as it creates positive communication channels between us and our dogs, so we can clearly communicate our needs to them and vice versa.

Dog training is as much about you, as it is your dog, so try not to get frustrated if your dog is not learning something as quickly as you think they should, it is more likely that you may be the one not doing things quite right, or not being clear with your communication which could slow down your progress, but the whole aim is to learn together. If your dog is particularly struggling with learning a new behaviour, try and simplify the exercise for the them to increase their chances of success, then build up from there. This will avoid frustration building and also increase their confidence as they will feel good when they are being rewarded for doing something correctly.

Training sessions are better being kept shorter where possible, I usually aim for around 10 minutes at a time but this will vary for each individual dog, as this will keep their interest levels high and their enthusiasm flowing. Remember, training is a hugely mentally stimulating process, particularly when your dog is learning something new from scratch, so it is understandably very tiring for them. Allow for plenty of rest and sleep breaks in-between training, so any new learning can be processed more effectively. Training sessions are about sculpting desirable behaviours and this can only be done if your dog is ready to learn, but sometimes just like us humans, they may be having a bit of bad day, they may be tired, hungry or feeling under the weather, meaning training is much less likely to go well. If you dog seems disinterested, simply give them a break and go back to it later, when you are likely to achieve better results.

Remember, whenever possible to set your dog up for success and also to end your sessions on a positive note to keep them wanting more. I would rather my dogs show me a behaviour really well just once or twice, rather than letting them carry on and risk them making mistakes.

Many people say all too often, 'I don't have time for this amount of training', but I can assure you that you really do. You would be surprised how many training opportunities there are in a day! Whilst you are waiting for the kettle to boil, whilst the microwave is warming your lunch, in the advert breaks of your favourite TV programme or whilst you are waiting for the bath to run are all golden opportunities to squeeze in mini training sessions. In fact, most of the party tricks my dogs know have been taught to them in these few minute bursts over a few days. The key is to keep the sessions fun, short and positive and repeating them consistently for a guaranteed way to enable you to see the desired results.

A common trap that many owners fall into, is simply repeating verbal cues several times and their dog appearing to ignore them. This is actually more likely to be because your dog doesn't realistically know what they are being asked to do. Although 'Delta, Heel' seems like a clear enough instruction to us humans, unless your dog has actually been taught what those words mean, it is really nothing more than a pretty useless piece of background noise to them. Similarly, you should always be clear and consistent with the verbal cues you decide to use; as we all know, the English language is often confusing even for humans, so can you imagine how complex it must be for a dog to comprehend too? For example, you may say 'Sit Down' to ask your dog to sit, as well as 'Lie Down' to ask your dog to lie on the floor, as well as 'Get Down' to ask your dog to not jump up or to get off the sofa, but to your dog, they all pretty much sound and mean the same thing, so you can see how confusion soon arises. You may find it useful, particularly if you are just starting your training journey, to make a table of all the verbal cues you use, and what they look like to you. For example, 'Sit' means that your dog's bottom is on the floor, 'Down' means your dog lies down fully on the floor and 'Here' means your dog returns to you. If there are multiple members of your household then creating a list such as this can be a useful way to make sure everyone is singing from the same hymn sheet, so to speak, and using all the same terminology. It is also important to note that you should try and refrain from constantly saying your dog's name before your verbal ques, for example if I had one of my dogs sat in front of me and I already had their focus and attention on me, there would be little point in saying 'Delta, Sit,' then 'Delta, Down', then Delta, Paw' and so on, as using her name continually is unnecessary. I only really use my dog's names when I need to get their attention, as I am sure that if people constantly shouted my name all day for every single sentence that they said wanted to me, it would soon get extremely tiresome and I would likely start to ignore them. The same rule applies for your dog, so try to avoid the over use of your verbal cues or your dog's name.

Considering the ethos behind positive reinforcement training, imagine if you had a boss, that constantly criticised your work, shouted at you in front of your colleagues and threatened to fire you, then that is unlikely to motivate you to work hard is it? However, if your boss praised you consistently and offered you pleasant incentives in return for reaching achievable goals, it is likely that that would motivate you to replicate and continue your good work in the future, in order for you to receive more positive feedback or rewards again. Training using intimidating or outdated methods will only ever be detrimental to the relationship you share with your dog long term.

I would always recommend to start teaching your dog new behaviours somewhere with minimal distractions to begin with, to give them the best chance of learning the behaviour successfully. The distractions can then be introduced gradually to 'proof' the behaviour in various different scenarios. We would not take our first driving lesson on a motorway, we are more likely to start off somewhere quiet where the risks are low, distractions are minimal and it is generally safer for us to learn and practice our new found skills. The same rules apply to our dogs. My favourite motto is 'set them up for success' and in order to do that, build your solid foundations for behaviours at home first, then practice them in quiet places, before expecting good results in areas with lots of distractions

Below are a couple of examples of basic behaviours that would be beneficial to teach your dog and how you would go about teaching them positively using clicker training;

Sit

An easier example to start with would be 'Sit.' Begin by luring your dog into the correct position by holding a treat in front of their nose and slowly moving it upwards above their head, you should hopefully find that they automatically go into a sitting position naturally. Then, as soon as your dog's bottom touches the floor into the sitting position, this is when you should click and reward. Don't worry about verbal commands in the early stages of new behaviours, these can be added in later once your dog better understands exactly what they are being asked to do.

Recall

I would consider this to be one of the most important things you need to teach your dog, not only to allow them freedom, but also for their own safety. Dogs are not born understanding the dangers they may face in our human focused world including traffic, roads, being stolen, hazardous environments etc so in order to let them off the lead, we need them to come back to us. Recall training should be started as early as possible, within your home and garden first where there are fewer distractions. To teach this using clicker
training, start by calling your dog's name and the second they turn to look at you, click and reward. It is important to mark the exact point in which your dog decides to stop what they are doing, and then actively choose to come to interact with you, as this is the basis of a solid recall. At this point, if you have introduced the clicker correctly, then your dog should be associating the click meaning they have a reward on the way from you, so they should therefore seek you out to claim their prize. Once this is becoming cemented, you can then add a verbal cue such as 'Come' or 'Here' provided that the same word is used consistently each time.

Leave

Teaching your dog to leave successfully is an essential life skill for them to have included in their training repertoire. Dogs naturally explore new things with their noses and often that can lead to them exploring further by picking things up, which ordinarily is not a problem in itself. However, if they pick something up that is potentially hazardous to them such as a sharp piece of litter when they are out on their walk, or something which could be poisonous to them such as chocolate, then it is imperative that they know how to leave this when they are asked to do so. Owners often overlook this behaviour and do not realise the importance of it until their dog is already in danger. The key to teaching a successful 'leave' is to make sure that you are essentially asking your dog to swap the item, for something of much higher value. Therefore, you need your best treats or most exciting toys for this one, to really get your dog's attention. Start by allowing your dog to pick something up, like a toy for example, then, excitedly offer them your tasty treat, as soon as their mouth opens to drop the item, you need to click and reward them with the said treat. Once they have mastered this, you can add the verbal cue of 'leave' or 'drop' for example, so they then begin to associate this cue with the action of physically opening their mouths to drop the item.

Muzzle

As we will go on to discuss in the Veterinary Care & Complementary Therapies chapter, muzzle training can be hugely beneficial for any dog to learn. Even usually friendly amenable dogs, can behave out of character when they are under extreme stress or in pain, so it is common practice for veterinary professionals to put a muzzle on your dog to avoid any bite injuries to themselves whilst they are treating them. Training your dog to accept and wear a muzzle comfortably will mean that they will not then have the added stress of wearing this alien piece of equipment when they have already found themselves in a stressful situation.

There are also other reasons why dogs may need to be muzzled on a day-to-day basis including if they show aggression towards other dogs or people or if they are known to scavenge food from the floor outside which may be dangerous if they ingest it.

This should be done alongside training however and care must be taken to not put your dog in a situation where they have to resort to a bite, even though they are wearing a muzzle.

Teaching your dog to wear a muzzle should be a slow and calm process that is not rushed, to avoid creating any negative feelings from your dog surrounding the muzzle. Start by simply showing your dog the muzzle, click and reward. Once they are happy with sniffing the muzzle you may try putting it over the very end of their nose, click and reward. You may find it useful to spread some meat paste, dog safe peanut butter or cheese spread on the inside end of the muzzle, so your dog can lick this off and associate the muzzle with this tasty reward. Repeat this until they are comfortable and carry on in a similar way until their full snout is in the muzzle, click and reward. Finally pass the muzzle straps behind your dog's head without physically fastening it, click and reward. Repeat again until they are comfortable then fasten it for a matter of seconds, click and reward. These foundations can then be built upon until your dog is happy to wear the muzzle. This by any means, does not have to be all done in one training session, in fact it is likely to take a lot longer but it is better to go slowly to desensitise them to wearing one, than to rush and make them fearful of wearing it. Delta wears a muzzle when she is out on walks, due to her lack of confidence around new dogs and people, and she is happy to have it put on as she associates positively with it. It is important to note that the type of muzzle you use is different depending on the situation, so for every day exercise use, such as Delta's, you need a 'basket' muzzle which allows your dog to breathe and pant freely whilst they are exercising. Occlusion muzzles do not allow your dog to open their mouth whatsoever, so they should only be used for very short periods of time, for example whilst they are receiving emergency veterinary care and they are therefore not suitable for exercising your dog in.

Teaching Complex Behaviours

For more complex behaviours, you will benefit from breaking down the lessons into smaller, more manageable sections. If behaviours have increased in difficulty, so much so that your dog consistently fails to execute them correctly, then this is likely to increase their frustration levels and in turn make them even less likely to learn a new behaviour effectively. Remember, we should always aim to set our dogs up to succeed, so if you can see they are struggling with something, make it easier and build upwards from there. For example, teaching 'Roll over' would be more effective if it was split down into different elements;

- Ask your dog to lie down, click and reward.
- Lure your dog to lie on their side, using a treat on the end of their nose, click and reward.
- Repeat the first 2 steps.
- Once they are executing these steps efficiently,

you can then encourage them using treats to roll over, as soon as they go to roll you should click and reward.

- Verbal cues can then be added later on in the process once your dog knows exactly what you are asking them to do.

The vast majority of assistance dogs, medical detection dogs, sniffer dogs, police dogs, guide dogs and therapy dogs are all trained using positive reinforcement techniques, which is motivating for pet dog owners that there are literally thousands of behaviours you can teach to your dog, if you can think of it, you can most probably teach it! From party tricks, to cooperative care techniques or to teach them how to help you around the house, this can all be achieved by positive reinforcement training. You can even let your dog suggest new behaviours for them to learn in a process known as 'Shaping' or 'Free Clicking' which is where you simply allow your dog to exhibit whatever behaviour they want, then when you see something you would like them to do more of, you immediately click and reward. This is a technique I use a lot with my own dogs, as they already have an excellent understanding of clicker training and how it works to their advantage. This technique also enables you to teach your dog tricks that are more personal to them, for example, Delta is a naturally vocal dog who often growls, grunts and barks so I started to click every time she made a particular quiet bark and rewarded it. I then introduced the verbal cue of 'Speak' so that is a trick she essentially already knew, that she now does when she is asked. I use the phrase 'What else can you do?' to let the dogs know that this is the time to think for themselves and offer up any behaviours they like, to see if I like them too! This often results in them going through any trick they can possibly think of, in order to gain access to their reward, then when they have exhausted all those options, they start offering up new behaviours just in case they will get rewarded for those too.

Professional Help

There is also no shame in feeling overwhelmed by your dog's behaviour and training and feeling the need to reach out for professional help. However, as with dog walkers and day-care providers, the world of dog training and behaviour is totally unregulated, meaning anyone can set up as a canine behaviourist or trainer, even if they have no relevant experience. Therefore, care must be taken to ensure anyone you employ to help you, whether that be the trainer at the puppy classes you attend, or the behaviourist that visits your home, or the trainer of the group classes you are considering, even the online seminars available to you, all follow positive reinforcement techniques. After all, there really is no excuse to let anybody bully or intimidate your dog and force them into uncomfortable situations or recommend cruel equipment to you as this is almost guaranteed to cause more harm than good and damage the relationship you share with your dog.

Problems that are recognised early are much more easily remedied, so asking for help if you are out of your depth is the kindest thing you can do for your dog, as it is likely that a dog who is experiencing behavioural issues is often struggling day to day too.

Veterinary Care & Complementary Therapies

Throughout your dog's life, it is guaranteed that they will need to visit a Veterinary Surgery at some stage. It is a cliché that all dogs hate the vets and they have to be dragged in through the door, but it really doesn't need to be this way with some careful preparations and training. After all, considering that every time a dog goes to the vet, something unpleasant happens to them; they are injected, have their temperature taken, have a cold stethoscope on their chest to check their heart, they may have their blood taken requiring them to be restrained by one stranger whilst another invades their personal space to carry out the procedure and so on, so it is not hard to understand why they quickly develop negative feelings towards these types of situation that they find themselves in.

Many vets today offer 'Puppy Parties' where young pups can go and socialise with other puppies of a similar age inside the veterinary practice, which is a great way to acclimatise them to the unusual smells and sounds of a veterinary surgery. Some practices even offer social visits to further assist your puppy/dog with getting used to being in the veterinary environment, without anything unpleasant happening to them whilst they are there.

There are also steps you can take at home in order to make your dog more comfortable when they attend veterinary appointments. For example, getting them used to being handled in a similar way to how veterinary staff may handle them. You could encourage them to allow you to lift their gums gently to look at their teeth and reward them with treats and praise for allowing you to do so. Similarly, it is important that your dog can tolerate gentle handling of their body too, so reward them for allowing you to move your hands across their body, or them allowing you to lift their paws, or their tail. If at any point your dog is uncomfortable, this handling should be stopped, as you don't want to take any steps backwards with this.

As we mentioned earlier, you may also wish to consider teaching your dog how to wear a muzzle comfortably, in order to prepare them if an emergency situation were to unfortunately occur. It is common practice for vets to muzzle your dog, particularly when they are administering emergency treatment, as even the most placid, friendly dog can act out of character when they are in pain, in shock, highly stressed or frightened. Teaching your dog to wear a muzzle comfortably for this purpose, will mean that they have one less stressful encounter to deal with in an already stressful situation. To do so, you need to condition your dog to wearing a muzzle using positive reinforcement techniques, which is discussed in detail in the previous chapter on Positive Reinforcement Training. It is better to introduce this experience to your dog and never need to use it, than to wish you had taught your dog to be comfortable in a muzzle when they are already in the stressful situation.

In line with this advice, you should ensure that you choose a vet that you trust to not only have the expertise to treat your dog effectively, but also one that is going to treat them kindly. It is all very well and good you putting in the hard work preparing your dog to ensure they are comfortable being examined, but this ground work can rapidly be undone if your chosen vet does not show them the same kindness and patience when handling and treating them.

In relation to your dogs continued wellbeing and contentment, it is imperative that necessary treatment of any illnesses or injuries is done so as soon as is possible. Nobody knows your dog better than you do, so it is probable that you will notice anything being slightly wrong. Any health concerns should be raised with a veterinarian as soon as possible so your dog can receive the appropriate treatment promptly. It should also be noted that any sudden behavioural changes you see in your dog may indicate that they are in pain, so this should always be explored. Most reputable canine behaviourists will ask if your dog has been recently medically examined before agreeing to work with them, particularly if their behaviour change is recent.

Alongside conventional medical treatments and medications, it may also be beneficial to consider introducing some alternative therapies alongside their veterinary care. We shall look into some of the most common types of complementary therapies below:

Hydrotherapy – Hydrotherapy is a form of physiotherapy that utilises water resistance in order to relieve pain and rehabilitate injuries. This is a low impact exercise which is ideal for recovery and rehabilitation. This can be carried out in a swimming pool, in an underwater treadmill or using a whirlpool. Your dog's situation and their need for hydrotherapy treatment, will determine which of these options is the most suitable for them. Any hydrotherapist should be registered with the relevant bodies and in doing so, it ensures that the hydrotherapist conforms to a high standard of guidelines and that they will seek veterinary consent before beginning any treatment with your dog.

Massage – A non-invasive therapy that aims to help rehabilitate muscular injuries and provide support for long term conditions such as Arthritis. It is also worth considering massage if you regularly practice high intensity dog sports such as agility or flyball, to ensure any muscle strains are noticed in the early stages and to help keep your dog in peak physical condition. When my eldest two dogs were younger, we regularly competed in agility and flyball competitions and each month we had our team dogs checked over by a canine massage practitioner, so that any minor issues could be spotted in their early stages, to prevent them getting any worse, which was hugely beneficial. Basic massage techniques can also be a great way to help your dog relax too, so learning some of those for yourself is a useful skill to possess.

Physiotherapy – Most commonly, physiotherapy is used alongside veterinary treatment, usually following surgery to aid recovery. The aim it to restore movement and function to parts of the dog's body and also to prevent future secondary complications. It usually consists of several different exercises and techniques dependent on the dog's individual needs.

Laser Therapy – Laser therapy consists of infra- red radiation being directed onto damaged or inflamed areas of the body in order to promote and accelerate healing. It has been shown to have positive effects on issues such as Arthritis as well as a wide range of other illnesses.

Acupuncture – Acupuncture is when fine needles are inserted into specific points over the dog's body, known as Acupuncture Points, which is where nerves and blood vessels meet. The aim is to assist the body to heal itself by stimulating the repair mechanisms found in the dog's nervous system, immune system and hormonal system. This should only be carried out by a qualified practitioner but it is generally well tolerated by the majority of dogs.

Reiki – Although Reiki is one of the more alternative therapies mentioned, it has been shown to have positive effects. It is an ancient Japanese healing practice that involves the channelling of natural healing energies into your dog. It is used to reduce pain, promote relaxation, reduce stress and enhance your dog's wellbeing.

Zoopharmacognosy – Deriving from ancient Greek, 'Zoo' meaning animal, 'Pharmaco' meaning remedy and 'Gnosy' meaning knowing, it involves your dog self-medicating through plant extracts in the form of essential oils, macerate, clays, minerals and many more. The dog then selects the remedy they require and access it through easting, licking, inhaling or rubbing on to it. It has been shown that wild animals have an innate ability to self-select remedies for their illnesses or ailments, including plants, clays or other natural remedies. Although are dogs are no longer wild animals, it is possible that this ability to self-medicate remains with them today. The age old saying of 'dogs will eat grass to make them sick' proves this theory that they will seek out what they need to help them, often before we know anything is wrong. Zoopharmacognosy should only be done under the guidance of a qualified practitioner.

Magnets – Magnetic therapy dates back thousands of years and it is thought to reduce inflammation and in turn, pain, by increasing circulation. Whilst there is little scientific evidence on how exactly the magnets benefit your dog, there is extensive anecdotal evidence from people who have personally used it on themselves, dogs or horses. The most commonly available magnetic products include collars and coats and they are thought to reduce recovery time following injury and also assist in the management of long-term joint issues. All 4 of my dogs wear a magnetic collar all the time and I have noticed a huge difference in the two older girl's mobility, and I have also found them to be helpful with regards to Delta's anxiety levels too.

Supplements – There are vast amounts of supplementary products available on the market today, many of which have good success rates. There are many natural supplements available to aid a whole host of health issues and illnesses which includes products for:

- Joint and mobility care

- Maintaining skin and coat health

- Improving dental hygiene

- Reducing anxiety levels

- Reducing fears and phobias

- Controlling digestive or urinary issues

- Balancing hormone levels

Personally, I have used all of the above complementary therapies, both with my own dogs and with dogs we fostered, all with good levels of success. Although many of these techniques do not have a great deal of scientific evidence to support their success rates, there are high numbers of personal anecdotal evidence to show that they have worked in that given situation. As with any treatment, either medical or alternative, there are no guarantees that they will all work for every dog, even if they have similar sets of symptoms as each other. Our main aim as dog owners is to ensure our dogs health, wellbeing and contentment, so we should keep our minds open to the possibility of other techniques being beneficial to them, even if it is something we have not previously considered.

For example, my youngest dog Delta, was hand reared by myself from around 5 weeks old, after her mother, herself and her siblings were abandoned in a house when their owner moved out. Because of the stress they were all under and the squalid living conditions they found themselves in, tragically 7 of the 8 puppies died and their mother, who was not producing milk, showed no interest in her one remaining puppy, hence the decision was made to separate them and hand rear Delta. Because of the highly traumatic experiences she had been through in just her few weeks of being alive, and the fact that she had received little nutrition, she was extremely unwell. She was then diagnosed with

Distemper, which is a potentially fatal virus that attacks their gut, heart, lungs, brain, nervous system and immune system, often resulting extreme vomiting, diarrhoea, seizures and even death. It is sadly likely that her siblings died as a result of undiagnosed and untreated Distemper, before we were made aware of their desperate situation. Thankfully, due to routine vaccinations being introduced in the 1950's, Distemper is now relatively uncommon, but it is still a high risk in situations like Delta's, where puppies are bred without any care for health or wellbeing.

In order to aid her recovery further, alongside extensive veterinary care, I decided to try some complementary therapies as it seemed they were likely to do more good than harm and I felt Delta deserved every opportunity possible to recover. This began when she was around 16 weeks old, as she was still struggling to get enough rest and recovery time, due to her having frequent seizures which were understandably extremely draining for her. A trusted friend is an experienced Reiki practitioner, so she suggested she should see Delta for some sessions. Having never really experienced first-hand what Reiki was, I really had no idea what to expect, but decided to go ahead and keep an open mind. For the first 10 minutes of the session, Delta was her usual fidgety self, but slowly she began to relax, until she actually fell fast asleep. This was unheard of for her, as she was so nervous in new situations, that she was often on high-alert, so for her to fall asleep was a huge step. We also attended sessions with a Zoopharmacognosy practitioner, who offered Delta a selection of essential oils, for her to self- select. She opted for the oils which related to trauma, stress and anxiety which made complete sense given her background of traumatic experiences. At this point, she was just under 12 months old and was still exceptionally nervous of new people and situations, but after licking the oils and macerates, she took herself onto a rug in the middle of room and fell into a deep sleep. This actually made me cry because I could not believe how this little dog who was so full of stress and anxiety, could relax enough to sleep in a totally new environment, it was truly magical and a moment I will never forget. We also went to weekly hydrotherapy sessions for around 12 months, to build her muscles and improve how she walked, as she was very unsteady and tired extremely easily which were a monumental help to her. A combination of veterinary treatments and complimentary therapies helped to save Delta's life and give her back some semblance of normality to her, for which I will always be truly grateful.

Grooming

Every dog needs to be groomed, whether that is by yourself at home or by attending regular appointments at a grooming salon. Even dogs that are thought to shed little to no hair, will still need to be groomed regularly to avoid any knots or tangles forming in their coat. Grooming also provides a great opportunity to highlight any issues your dog may have, that are not always apparent at first glance, such as fleas, ticks, cuts, sores, warts and even lumps which may be ordinarily hidden by your dog's coat. It is also of particular importance to dogs that suffer from skin issues that they are regularly groomed, to help keep a close eye on their skin and keep it in optimum condition.

However, it should be noted that excessive grooming can actually cause issues as well, as particularly if your dog is shampooed and washed too often, it can strip the coat of their natural oils, thereby drying out the coat and skin which can lead to irritations. I personally very rarely bath any of my dogs, unless they have rolled in something offensive, but even then, I try to just rinse that area clean, but I do brush them all regularly. Also, the use of chemically perfumed shampoos, sprays and scents may also lead to skin irritations for your dog and it is often why they take the first opportunity they have to roll in something after being groomed, to rid themselves of the artificial smells which may smell pleasant to us, but likely to be offensive to their sensitive noses.

Whether bathing your dog at home or taking them to a groomer, try to opt for hypoallergenic natural shampoos and products where possible, as these are less likely to cause any unwanted issues as they are kinder and gentler to the dog's coat and skin.

For certain breeds, grooming is even more important for them and it may actually become a welfare issue if this need is not attended too. Particularly with longer haired breeds such as Shih-Tzus, Lhasa Apsos, Bearded Collies and Afghan Hounds, their grooming needs are much more demanding than those with short hair such as Smooth Haired Dachshunds, Jack Russells, Whippets and Greyhounds, simply because they have much more coat to contend with. Commonly, naturally long-haired breeds tend to sport short haircuts when they are not show dogs, simply because it is easier for their owners to deal with on a day-to-day basis, however if they do still have a full coat, regularly grooming is crucial. Long hair can quickly become tangled, knotted and matted, which in turn twists and pulls on the dog's skin which is uncomfortable for them and in severe cases can also impede their mobility. There have even been severe neglect cases where dogs have lost tails or limbs due to excessive matting restricting the blood flow to those areas after their owners failing to groom them for extended periods of time.

For breeds that you know are likely to require regular professional grooming, it is important that you prepare them for this process as much as possible, so that they do not become stressed by it. This is where is it beneficial to get your dog comfortable with basic grooming techniques at home before expecting them to tolerate them at a salon. Ensuring the groomer, you choose to use, practices kind handling and is patient is also imperative. Those who use physical force or intimidation to get the grooming done should be avoided at all costs, and many groomers are happy for you to watch them groom before deciding to take your dog to them. By keeping on top of your dog's grooming schedule as much as possible between professional grooms you will not only make life easier for your groomer, but will also avoid any unnecessary stress for your dog when they need to have several matts shaved off them which may be uncomfortable for them.

For dogs who enjoy the grooming process, it can

actually be a great way to get them to relax and de- stress, and strengthen the bond that they share with you. I have known dogs personally who actually fall asleep because they find being brushed so relaxing! Although this is not the case for every dog, there are steps you can take to help your dog form more positive associations with being brushed, by practicing it regularly and rewarding them for remaining calm. Choosing the most suitable grooming equipment can make this process easier however, so it important to carefully consider the types of brushes and combs that would be most suitable for your dog's coat length and type. For double coated breeds that have a dense undercoat as well as a topcoat, they may benefit from an 'Undercoat Rake' style brush which is designed to remove dead undercoat, without damaging the topcoat. Breeds with double coats include; Huskies, Pomeranians and Labrador Retrievers. A common mistake that owners make is to shave their double coated dog's fur during warmer weather, as they are concerned about them overheating, however this is likely to actually make them warmer and leave them vulnerable to sun damage, as their coat is designed to keep them cool.

Your dog's nails often go unnoticed day-to-day, but they actually play a very important role in your dog's mobility. In extreme cases, where the dog does not have the opportunity to wear their nails down naturally by walking on hard ground or digging, they can become so long that they can actually begin to curve back around and dig into the underside of their pads which would be excruciatingly painful for them. Thankfully, this would only happen in extreme cases of neglect, so you are unlikely to see this occur in your own dog, however even if your dog's nails are allowed to get a little bit too long, this can still be detrimental to them as it puts pressure on their toes and pads, which in turn affects their leg joints and mobility. For the majority of breeds, you should not be able to hear your dog's nails tapping on hard floors when they walk, and the nail itself should not be touching the floor when they are stood still. If either of these are apparent, it is likely that the nails would benefit from being trimmed.

Care must be taken when trimming your dog's nails at home, to not damage the soft tissue and blood vessels which run through the nail known as the 'quick.' For dogs who have lighter nails, the quick is usually easy to see but this can be more difficult to distinguish with dogs who have dark nails. Cutting a nail too short and in turn damaging the quick, will not only cause the quick to bleed but it will also create a negative association of the nail clippers causing pain to your dog, so they are likely to be less tolerant of the process happening in the future. Particularly with dogs whose nails have not been cut for a long time, the quick is also likely to be longer, so you are better to trim small amounts of the nail over a few days or weeks as opposed to trying to cut them short straight away and risking damage. Nail trimming can also be carried out by your dog groomer or veterinary staff members, if it is not possible for you to do it yourself at home.

There are also other options available if you would prefer to not use the traditional nail clippers including scratch boards and nail grinders. Scratch boards can easily be made at home by fastening sand paper to a wooden board, or if you prefer you can purchase a ready-made one instead. The aim here is to teach your dog to scratch the board, as the name suggests, which will gradually wear down their nails into a natural shape. This also doubles up as trick training, so not only will it help maintain your dog's nails, it will also provide them with mental stimulation at the same time, as they are learning a new behaviour.

Nail grinders are essentially small motorised tools with a rotating grinder at the end of them, which can be used to wear down your dog's nails. When they are introduced and used correctly, they can be a very useful tool to maintain the length of your dog's nails, whilst minimising the risk of damaging the quick. However, many of them are noisy when they are in operation and so you will need to introduce them to your dog using positive reinforcement training techniques. You could start by simply allowing your dog to sniff the nail grinder without it being switched on, then click and reward them for showing an interest and remaining calm. This can then progress to it being turned on and again, click and reward for them remaining calm. Once they are comfortable with this, you can hold their paw and move the nail grinder towards the nail without making contact, click and reward. Finally make contact with the nail with the nail grinder, click and reward. This process may take several sessions and may even need to be broken down further into more achievable sections, depending on how sensitive your dog is to noises and new experiences, but persevere and be patient.

Regular grooming sessions also provide you with the opportunity to check for other issues that may be in the early stages of development with your dog, which can then be highlighted to a veterinarian more rapidly. Use this time to check your dog's eyes, which should be clear and bright, with no signs of discharge or dryness. Their eyelashes should not be curling in towards the eye and if they are, they may be suffering from a condition known as Entropion, in which their eyelids and lashes fold inwards and then rub on the eyeball, often causing ulcers, and it is extremely painful. Their nose should ideally be wet, but not running, nor should it be excessively dry or cracked. Some dog's noses are naturally dryer than others, so get to know what is usual for your dog, as a dry nose is not always necessarily indicative of illness. Their ears should be clean inside and this is particularly important to keep track of in those breeds who have droopy ears such as Basset Hounds, as they can get dirt and moisture trapped inside them more easily than those with pricked ears so they therefore may be more prone to developing ear infections as well as conditions such as ear mites, which cause a brown gunky substance to form inside the ear canal which is often very itchy. Finally, if they are comfortable doing so, check their teeth for any signs of damage or a build-up of tartar. Puppies should have a full set of 28 teeth, with adult dogs having 42 once they have finished teething and lost all of their puppy teeth by around 8 months of age. It is also worth noticing what your dog's normal gum colour is, as if this suddenly becomes pale it can indicate shock or bleeding, if they are a darker red it usually indicates inflammation within the gum and mouth or if they have a yellowish tinge to them, known as jaundice, it can be a sign of liver issues. All of these findings should be explored further by a veterinarian.

Another important part of your dog's grooming which also often goes unnoticed, is their whiskers on their faces. These are scientifically known as 'vibrissae' and these are long, thick hairs that are usually found on their faces, around the jaw, above the eyes and around their mouths. Care must be taken to ensure that these are not trimmed down or even cut off completely as they are an essential part of your dog's sensory system. Any touch or air movement on or around your dog's whiskers, stimulates the nerves found in the base of them which in turn sends signals to their brain. This not only helps them to better navigate their environment, but it also reduces the risk of them being injured as the whiskers are often the first part of the body to notice something being near to their face. For example, if the whiskers around the eye are touched, this makes your dog blink, which could avoid something potentially damaging entering the eye such as twigs or airborne debris.

Some groomers and owners trim of remove the whiskers for aesthetic purposes and whilst it would not cause your dog pain to have their whiskers trimmed, as they do not contain pain receptors, it is not recommended due to the detriment it can cause them by removing this extra method of sensing their environments.

Accepting The Dog You Have

This is a topic that is very close to home for me, as it took me a long time to fully accept Delta's behaviour and personality traits and she really opened my eyes to how other owners truly feel when their dog does not fit into social normality. We most commonly bring dogs into our lives for the companionship that they offer us, but sometimes a dog comes along that is a lot more complex than previous dogs we have shared our lives with and it can be hard to accept this and know how to deal with it appropriately.

We have previously touched on Delta's story in the Socialisation and Habituation Chapter as well as the Veterinary Care and Complementary Therapies Chapter, but her story is long and complicated enough to easily fill her own book. However, I felt it necessary to include a brief insight into her life with me as I hope it is likely to benefit other owners in similar situations to make them realise that they are not alone.

I like to think that I have raised my older three Border Collies successfully, though they all came to me at different ages and from very different backgrounds, however they have all turned out pretty well. They are all generally sociable, friendly dogs who are comfortable in the vast majority of situations they find themselves encountering in day-to-day life. However, even though Delta is the same breed as my other girls and I bought her up in exactly the same way and using the same methods as the others, she is most definitely different and she struggles a lot with anxiety, particularly when facing new encounters. She is what is now known in the dog training world as a 'Reactive' dog meaning that she often reacts negatively to other dogs, people, objects or situations she finds herself in. For us, that meant that she was unable to enjoy many of the things that my other girls enjoyed, simply because her anxiety was so heightened.

For a long time, I felt guilty that her life was nowhere near as 'normal' as the rest of my dogs, and felt I had let her down. I felt sad that she would never feel comfortable enough around other dogs to play with one in the park, or that she would likely never feel confident enough around strangers to join me at a dog-friendly coffee shop. Needless to say, I shed a lot of tears because I was so desperate for her to lead a normal life, following her horrendous start, however, in reality, there are lots of factors that have altered Delta's behaviour that were totally beyond my control.

Delta's main triggers are other dogs, particularly when they are off lead and she is on lead, as well as strangers approaching her, children who make high pitched noises, the beep the machine makes when someone delivers a parcel and the sound of a doorbell on the television. All of these encounters create her high levels of anxiety and she often shows this by repetitively barking, with her hackles up which could be seen as aggression. However, as I know that this reaction is stemmed from intense anxiety, it would be inappropriate to punish her, simply for her being scared. Almost daily I discover more things that cause her anxiety and they are often things that you would not expect. On one of our recent walks, whilst we take care to choose routes that allow us to avoid other people and dogs where possible, Delta suddenly started fearfully barking and it turns out the cause was actually a bench! She was genuinely terrified of the bench, but with some careful encouragement and ample amounts of tasty treats, she soon tentatively approached it and quickly sniffed it, before being brave enough to walk past it. This situation is something my other dogs would take in their stride, as would the vast majority of dogs, however, it is not until you have a dog that is potentially frightened of anything, that you truly notice your immediate surroundings, in order to adjust them accordingly where possible to make sure your dog feels safe.

I have now accepted that Delta will likely never be as comfortable with the outside world as my other dogs and whilst large amounts of training and confidence building exercises have certainly improved things for her, they have by no means 'fixed' how she feels when she encounters things outside the comfort of her own home. We are at a stage now where this is totally acceptable and instead of focussing solely on attempting to make her like things that she is fearful of, that cause her distress, we look instead for new things to try which she may enjoy.

Even the most well-intentioned new owner, who has done extensive research into their chosen breed, or an owner who is very experienced in a particular breed having owned them for many years can be taken back by an individual dog that is not what they were expecting or previously used to. This can be extremely difficult to accept, particularly if this means that the life you had planned with your dog, then has to change to better accommodate them. Having a dog that is often so crippled by their own anxieties and fears can be a very lonely situation to be in and for me it felt as if literally every other dog we saw was the happy-go-lucky dog that I wanted Delta to be. Luckily for me, my other dogs, particularly Inka is the kind of dog you can only dream of, that is happy no matter what she is faced with, so she is able to accompany me wherever I go. Though I imagine for someone who has just one dog, with similar issues to those Delta has, it would be easy to feel overwhelmed and isolated when it seems you must avoid every other living being, to keep your dog from feeling excessively anxious and scared.

Whilst my experience with Delta is centred around her reactivity, there are also many other reasons why the plans you had for your dog's life may change. For example, you may actively compete in agility and when you decide to add another dog to your life in order to continue this, the dog you have may unfortunately be diagnosed with hip dysplasia therefore rendering them unable to do competitive agility as planned. Now you have one of two options here, you either choose to rehome them as they are not the dog you envisioned and they cannot compete in agility as you intended, or you accept that this is the case and decide to explore an alternative lower impact sport, such as obedience or scentwork, thereby allowing your dog to lead a happy, healthy life, all be it different to the one you set out to achieve. I know which one I would pick! As with any dog sport, your dog should always be a companion to you first that you love unconditionally, and then anything else that they achieve should be a bonus, not the be all and end all.

Another example may be a litter of puppies that have been carefully bred and selected to complete intensive training programmes to make them an assistance dog of some kind. Unfortunately, no matter how carefully their genetics are considered, or how suitable they may appear to be on paper, in reality, not every dog will pass through the training with ease. For those that continually struggle, it should be questioned whether it is fair to them to continually set them up to fail and even potentially put a person's life at risk if they only just scrape through the training requirements, or instead if they should be rehomed to a 'pet' home instead of a working one, where they are likely to live a happier, more contented life.

For us to continually put our dogs in situations that we know affects their mental health negatively, simply because that is what we wanted to do with them, would be cruel. So we should always be open to compromise or even change our plans entirely to prioritise our dog's happiness instead.

All things considered, Delta has definitely made me a better dog owner and opened up a world of possibilities that I otherwise would not have explored without her coming into my life so for that, I am truly grateful. So, if your dog is not exactly as you imagined, it is important to remember that the more difficult, complex dogs often are the ones that teach us the most, so don't give up on them. Accepting the dog that you have is a huge step towards making your dog's life more content, as well as your own, as they do not have to contend with the high levels of stress they would encounter if you continually forced them into situations that they are uncomfortable with.

Myth Busting

There are so many myths and misconceptions still flying around the canine world, so it is all too easy to get drawn into following incorrect, outdated and sometimes even dangerous advice. Thankfully in today's society, there is a strong shift towards positive training methods with the dog's wellbeing at the heart of it, however unfortunately there are still many 'professionals' practicing training and behaviour modification using harsh, cruel methods which is certainly not a route we want to be travelling down with our beloved companions.

The best piece of advice I can provide you with is to 'work with the dog you have in front of you.' This really is crucial if you are concerned about making your dog's life as happy and contented as possible. Placing unrealistic expectations on your dog is only ever going to set you both up for failure, instead of success. As intelligent as dogs are, they are not born with an innate understanding of what we want them to do or how we want them to behave, so it is therefore our job to teach them in a kind and effective way, which we looked at further at in the Positive Reinforcement Training Chapter earlier in the book.

Below are a few of the most common theories and beliefs that still plague the world of dog ownership and training, which have all now been disproven thanks to advances in research and continued scientific studies;

Dominance – Contrary to popular belief, your dog will not try and take over the world if you let them sit alongside you on the sofa or lie next to you in bed! Dominance is actually very much a fluid state, which applies more to dog-to-dog interactions. Dogs are naturally much more inclined to avoid confrontation than to actively start any conflict, so in one situation they may appear dominant (i.e., taking a bone from another dog) and in another they may appear submissive (i.e., giving up their toy to another dog) This is not to say that this situation would play out in the exact same way, every time they occur. It all depends on how much they value the item at that particular time.

It is also important to note that our domestic dogs are not wolves, nor do they behave like them, so to treat them as such is unfair. Practicing physical acts of dominance on your dog with things like 'Alpha Rolls,' in which you use physical force to roll your dog onto their side, to make them 'submit' and to show your dominance over them, will in fact cause them huge amounts of emotional distress. Although a dog which has been 'Alpha

Rolled' may appear to have calmed down or be submissive, it is actually much more likely that they have shut down, in order to avoid any further violence. This is a built-in survival tool that our dogs have in order to appease attackers, or those showing them aggression to avoid any potential further injuries.

Within this dominance theory, there are a couple of other common myths which need to be set straight. Firstly, rubbing your dog's nose into their own urine or faeces if they have an accident in the house will not stop them from doing it again. What it will do however, is instil fear in them which you would then be the cause of. Naturally, dogs are very clean animals, this is demonstrated from an early age when the Mother dog cleans up her 'den' and her puppies whenever they urinate or defecate, so most dogs would be very reluctant to relieve themselves in their own space. Puppies especially, simply cannot hold their bladder and bowels for very long at all, so it is our job as their owner to make sure they have very regular opportunities to relieve themselves outside and that they are highly rewarded for doing so. This is also the case for older dogs, who as they age, often do not have the same bladder and bowel control they had when they were younger. As frustrating as it is for us humans, at such a young age, a puppy simply does not understand the difference between urinating on your carpet, as opposed to going on the grass outside and when they have to go, they have to go! Similarly, if owners return back home to find their dog has had an accident, it may well have happened a few hours previously, so chastising or punishing for them will have no relevance to the dog as they will not understand why you are shouting at them.

Pack Leader – There are still several well-known 'dog-trainers' who actively encourage you to behave as a pack leader over your dog, which science has now proved to be ineffective and is instead actually more likely to be detrimental to your relationship with their dog, as well as to their wellbeing.

For example, one trainer who unfortunately is still very popular on television, claims that when you walk your dog, for the first 15 minutes the dog should not be allowed to sniff, or relieve themselves, or walk in front of you whatsoever. If they do walk in front of you, or the lead has any tension at all, then a correction should be made by pulling back sharply on the lead. Only once they have obeyed these rules, they are rewarded by being allowed to sniff and urinate or defecate. Not only is this totally unnecessary, it is also cruel. Your dog's walk should be for them, not for you to demonstrate power over them!

They also actively suggest feeding your dog after you eat, and go on to encourage you to give your dog their food, then take it away from them just to prove that you are the pack leader and can take their food away. This can in fact increase the risk of your dog developing food aggression, as they never know when their food may be removed from them. I am sure we as humans would be equally unimpressed if we were served a meal, began to eat it, then had it removed from us with no valid reason. When you word it like that, it sounds ridiculously unfair and frustrating doesn't it?

This same trainer also advocates the use of shock collars and prong collars which again are outdated, cruel and do nothing except cause your dog to live in fear of you, as opposed to you building a strong, happy partnership based on trust. Although these methods may actually appear to show the results you are looking for, this is likely because your dog is afraid, or even shutting down, which surely is not morally the result anyone would want. Bullying your dog into subservience is not beneficial for either of you.

Collars – There is a common myth that all dogs should be walked on a collar, as 'harnesses encourage your dog to pull more,' however there is now evidence to prove otherwise. Dogs are naturally likely to pull, quite simply because they cover the ground faster than we do and we often walk much slower than their usual pace. It is actually quite unnatural for your dog to walk consistently by your side, without any tension on the lead and without deviating from this position. Equipment such as choke chains or slip leads, which were formally common place and very popular, are now considered as aversive, as they inflict discomfort and pain on a dog in order to achieve the desired results of your dog not pulling. For a dog that pulls a lot, or naturally walks in front of you, even a plain collar can be considered aversive, particularly if it worn high up the dog necks as this creates tension on their delicate neck area which is full of nerves and soft tissues which can be easily damaged. In many situations, a well fitted harness, which does not restrict your dog's natural movement, is a more appropriate choice for the comfort and safety of your dog, alongside positive training to teach them to walk well on a lead.

Reinforcing Fear – There is a myth surrounding this subject that you can reinforce your dog's fear by providing them with reassurance when they are frightened or anxious of a particular situation. It was previously suggested that for example, if your dog is afraid of fireworks, you should ignore them and let them sort themselves out so as not to reinforce their anxious behaviour. However, it is now much more commonly accepted that in fact the opposite is more likely to be true. Whilst it is important to not over-crowd your dog, or force them to interact with you when they are scared, if they seek your reassurance then it would not be detrimental for you to provide them with some comfort.

Punishment – Punishment is not as cut and dry as what may automatically spring to mind. Most people associate punishment with something bad happening to your dog as a result of their behaviour, and whilst this is the case, there are also other different variants to consider known as the 'Quadrants' of training; Positive Punishment, Negative Punishment, Positive Reinforcement and Negative Reinforcement. In the dog training world 'positive' means the addition of something and 'negative' means the removal of something. 'Punishment' relates to the behaviour reducing in frequency, whereas 'Reinforcement' means the behaviour increases in frequency. So, Positive Punishment is when something unpleasant is introduced to the dog in order to reduce the frequency of a behaviour, for example, using a choke chain which is uncomfortable and tight around their neck, to stop your dog pulling on the lead. Negative Punishment is the removal of something from the dog to reduce the frequency of their behaviour, for example, your dog barks at you for attention, so you turn away from them or leave the room completely to remove the attention they are demanding, thereby reducing the barking. Positive Reinforcement is what forms the basis of the most effective, ethical training methods as we discussed at length in the Positive Reinforcement Training Chapter and this is the process of adding something pleasant to the situation in order to increase the frequency of a behaviour and an example would be rewarding your dog with a tasty high value treat when they show a desired behaviour.

Negative Reinforcement is when something unpleasant is removed from the dog in order to increase a desired behaviour and an example would be when a dog is forced into a sitting position by a hand pushing them down, this hand is then removed when they are in the sitting position.

Where possible, punishment whether positive or negative, should be avoided and instead focus should be put onto the reinforcement options as this is not only better for your dog's mental wellbeing, it has also been shown to have more effective, long-lasting results.

Clever Dogs Are Easy To Train – Whilst it is true that breeds that are deemed as more intelligent, are easy to train, they also pick up a whole host of undesirable traits just as fast as they can learn good ones. Unfortunately, Border Collies often fall foul to this myth as first-time dog owners often think they would be better getting a very intelligent dog to make their training life easier. That is all well and good provided that you genuinely put in the vast amount of time and effort into guiding your dog to make good choices, and don't instead just rely on their own in-built intelligence to do the work for you. Breeds that are seen to have higher intelligence levels such as the Border Collies, the Golden Retrievers and the German Shepherds often require much higher levels of mental stimulation to avoid them getting bored or frustrated, so this should be considered carefully before opting for these breeds.

Teaching Old Dogs New Tricks – The old saying of 'You can't teach an old dog new tricks' is in fact completely untrue. Put simply, dogs learn about our world from the moment they are born, so they are never too old, or indeed too young, to start learning something new. So much so, as your dog ages it may mean that they are able to tolerate less physical exercise than their younger years, so teaching them tricks can enrich their lives more and provide them with some much-needed mental stimulation too.

Training Using Rewards Is Just Bribery – This is a common misconception in the world of dog training, particularly common in those that are new to positive reinforcement training, or those who still used more outdated, forceful methods. Using high value rewards such as treats and toys, does not bribe your dog into showing desirable behaviours, it simply rewards them for doing so, thereby increasing the likelihood of them displaying them again in the future. Many of us go to work and work hard every day; you don't do this because you are being bribed by the payday that awaits you at the end of the month, you are instead rewarded for the hard work you put in with money which you have earned. I would imagine that if this financial reward was removed and we no longer got paid to work, many of us would no longer be motivated to try hard or even show up to our jobs at all! This is the same concept for our dogs, they are more motivated to try hard and show desirable behaviours repetitively if they are rewarded well for doing so, so always make sure you pay well with your rewards.

My Dog Ignores Me – Whilst it may often feel like your dog is actively choosing to ignore you, what is more likely to be is happening is that they either do not know what you are asking them to do, or have something more interesting to focus their attention on. For example, if you are asking your dog to sit when they are surrounded by interesting distractions, and you simply keep repeating the same word over and over again, it is likely that your dog will quite simply switch off and find something else more engaging to do. Always try to set your dog up for success and encourage them to make appropriate choices, but don't expect the impossible for them. If your dog seems to be struggling to execute a behaviour that you think they actually know, you either need to revisit the training to ensure it is really cemented, or make their situation easier and less complex for them to show the behaviour properly.

My Dog Bit Me/Someone For No Reason – Put simply, there is always a reason that your dog would ever bite you or someone else and this would always be a last resort for them when they feel like they have no other option but to do so. What is more likely to have been the case, is that the person who was bitten, has failed to recognise the dog's discomfort for some time, resulting into this escalating into a bite. More subtle signals such as lip licking, avoiding eye contact and yawning are used to indicate your dog is uncomfortable in a situation and when these are ignored, they then go onto display more obvious signs such as a stiffening of their body, tailed tucked underneath them, ears pinned back and again if these are also ignored, they may feel they have no other choice but to growl, snarl, snap and eventually bite in order to get out of the situation they feel so threatened and uncomfortable in. The only known exception to this would be in the case of dogs with severe neurological issues, which may make their behaviour much more erratic or difficult to manage successfully, though this is relatively rare and a much more complex situation than that of an 'average' dog.

My Dog Must Go For Walks – Whilst there is often a large amount of social pressure to get out and walk your dog, this is not always a viable or suitable option. As we discussed in the Exercise chapter there are times when your dog may actually benefit from a rest day and skipping a walk and enjoying some enrichment and mental stimulation instead. This is particularly beneficial if you have a reactive dog that cannot process with the outside world as well as other dogs, to give them time for their stress levels to return back to a more manageable level.

Dogs Are Colour-blind – It is not true that our dogs can only see in black in white, but they do not see the world quite as we do. Human eyes usually have 3 colour receptor cones which allow us to see the full range of colours including different shades of each one. However, some humans are missing the colour receptor cone which recognises red and green colours, which is thought to be the same for our dogs. Because of this, dogs cannot recognise reds or greens or a mix of either of these colours so that also includes purples, oranges or pinks. This may explain why some dogs love the traditionally yellow coloured tennis balls to play with, as they can easily be differentiated from their other toys which will mostly appear, brown, grey, white and black. It may be beneficial therefore to choose either blue or yellow coloured toys to use as training rewards, as they will be easier for your dog to recognise and associate positively with.

1 Human Year = 7 Dog Years- It has long been suggested that for every human year, that equals 7 'dog years' however this is a little more complex. A dog's size and breed should be considered as generally speaking, smaller breeds not only tend to take longer to mature but they also usually live longer than large breed dogs. This is also important to consider when training your dog, as different breeds will reach adolescence at different times which can make training more challenging due to the sudden influx of hormones surging round your dog's body. So, if your dog seems to have regressed with their training and behaviour, then it is likely they may have reached adolescence and are simply struggling to concentrate.

Certain Breeds Are More Aggressive - Unfortunately, the media plays a huge part in what people come to expect from certain breeds. Currently, their doggy victim of choice is the Staffordshire Bull Terrier, who are often painted to be an aggressive, volatile, untrustworthy breed which realistically couldn't be further from the truth. The fact of the matter is, any dog has the potential to be aggressive, they all have sharp teeth and the ability to bite so assumptions should not be made based on their breed alone.

I Have Owned Dogs All My Life, I Know What I Am Doing - We should always be open to learning new techniques or researching new information on how to best look after our dogs. Just because someone may have owned dogs for 40 years, does not necessarily mean that they are using the most up to date, kind methods in caring for their current dogs. It may be that they are of the opinion that they 'have always done things this way' but time moves on, more science is discovered, things are researched more extensively and there is more easily accessible information out there now than ever before. We only know what we know at the time, but that is not to say that we should switch off the opportunity to learn new things, particularly when this learning is likely to benefit your dog's life greatly.

Conclusion

Whilst it is clear that there are many important aspects to consider when it comes to our dogs continued happiness and wellbeing, it is apparent that more sustainable, long lasting results are achieved when all of the aspects are considered as a whole, as opposed to individually. To reiterate this point, it should not be expected that a dog whose owner provides them with the most expensive dog food on the market, but then leaves their dog alone regularly for 12 hours a day, would be experiencing contentment. Providing your dog with lavish amounts of one thing, only to deprive them of another area altogether, is not a recipe for success or happiness, which cements the wholesome approach I refer to. All of the topics mentioned in each chapter, should therefore be considered collectively to provide the greatest results.

Referring back to the 'Five Freedoms' we mentioned in the introduction, it is important to reiterate that these can easily be vastly improved upon to ensure your dog achieves high levels of sustained contentment throughout their lives, as opposed to just received the very minimum basic level of care to keep them functioning. There is a distinct difference between merely existing and really living and feeling alive and happy, so it is paramount that your aim is to always give your dog the opportunity to thrive, and not just get by with what little they have access to.

In summary, here are my top tips for achieving complete canine contentment:

- Let your dog behave like a dog as often as possible by letting them exhibit their intrinsically natural behaviours. Let them sniff, dig, bark, roll in mud, play fetch, whatever they want to do to make them happy.
- Offer them choices as much as possible, whether that is choosing where to sleep, choosing the route they take on walks, or even choosing whether they want to receive physical fuss can create a mutual respect between them and us.
- Set them up for success by teaching them how to navigate our human focussed world, using positive training methods. Teach them anything you want to in the process, the possibilities are truly endless.
- Let them play and be silly sometimes, their life does not always have to be structured or ruled by routines; sometimes they just want to seize the opportunity to enjoy themselves.
- Appreciate how much they mean to us, and how much we mean to them too. We are their

world and they look to us for everything so don't underestimate that.

- Spend time with them, as much time as you can, go on adventures and be present in the moment with them. Their lives are undeniably short and you don't want to regret missed opportunities you wish you had shared with them.
- Always be kind to them. With your actions, with your words and how you treat them.
- Love them unconditionally despite their 'flaws.' It is often the most challenging dogs that teach us so much and our bonds with them can be even stronger because of this.

As we are all well aware, dogs are often considered as 'man's best friend' and they often go as far as to sacrifice their own happiness, in an attempt to improve ours, so it is our responsibility to ensure that we too are trying to improve our dog's lives, in the best ways we know how to. We ask them to sacrifice so much of themselves, simply by asking them to live alongside us, so it paramount that not only do they have ample opportunities to be themselves, but they also feel confident and comfortable enough to do so. Allowing your dog to truly express not only their most natural desires and behaviours, but also their own unique individual personalities, is guaranteed to pave the way for their happiness.

You are not required to invest copious amounts of money into making your dog happy, nor does it necessarily mean you are required to change every aspect of your life to fit around your dog, however you are undeniably required to invest a great deal of your time and patience if you are truly dedicated to improving your dog's life. Done correctly, having our dog living alongside us should actually enrich our own lives, as much as we enrich theirs. A happy dog is generally a much easier and more pleasurable dog to live alongside, which is set to benefit both them and us in equal measure.

Spreading awareness of your new found knowledge is also a fantastic step towards not only helping your own dog with feeling truly contented, but also to assist other owners on their canine journey too. Whether they are getting a dog for the first time, or even if they have had dogs for decades previously, there is never a bad time to learn new things and broaden their horizons and I can guarantee that their dogs will benefit just as much as your dog will.

So, upon reaching the end of this book, I am hopeful that you now feel better equipped with the knowledge you have gained to begin your journey of achieving complete canine contentment. The information found here forms the ideal foundations on which to build upon your dog's happiness, so the only thing that there is left to do now, is to get out there and put it into practice, I can guarantee your dog will thank you for it. After all, who doesn't want their dog to be as happy as they can possibly be?

Connect With The Author

If you have enjoyed reading my book and would like to keep in touch, you can find me on:

Facebook:
www.facebook.com/charlottegarnercanineauthor

Instagram:

@charlottegarnercanineauthor

Email: canineauthor@yahoo.com

If you have purchased the book through Amazon, I would really appreciate you leaving me a review on there too once you have finished reading it.

Or if you are reading the Kindle edition, I would appreciate you leaving me a star rating.

I would love to see photos of the lovely dogs you share your lives with and how this book may have benefitted them, so please feel free to send them to me via social media or email.

Thank you

Printed in Great Britain
by Amazon

17277349R00087